THE INSIDER
A TRUE STORY

Dan Verton

Llumina Press

ISBN: 1-59526-030-7

Printed in the United States of America by Llumina Press

Library of Congress Control Number: 2005904933

*To my wife, Corinne, and our little
ones, all of whom fill my life with
more joy than any one man deserves.*

Acknowledgements

My sincere thanks to the following people for their energy and professionalism in making this book happen:

Don Massaro and Kim Getgen of Reconnex Corp., for making their security experts available to me and sharing all that they could about the insider threat without betraying their customers' confidence; Mark Elster and Cynthia Kondratieff at Dolphin MultiMedia; Kristin Klitz, Molly Miller and the entire team at Engage PR; Andrew Tobias, for allowing me to quote from his great book on Charles Revson, *Fire and Ice*; the folks at Computerworld Magazine and Elizabeth Heichler, editor-in-chief of the IDG News Service, for allowing me to use their news stories for added context; to all of the federal and local law enforcement officials who shared their anecdotes with me at many a Secret Service meeting; Don Dickson, my boss and publisher of Homeland Defense Journal, for giving me the professional leeway to write and promote this book; and to Deborah Greenspan and her staff at Llumina Press for working with me on such an aggressive production schedule.

Be not too hasty to trust or to admire the teachers of morality…they discourse like angels, but they live like men.

— Samuel Johnson, *Rasselas*, 1759

CONTENTS

Author's Note

In March 2004, I gave a speech in California on the terrorist threat to critical infrastructures in the United States. It was based on the research that went into my last book, *Black Ice: The Invisible Threat of Cyber-Terrorism*. After the speech, I had the opportunity to talk with Don Massaro. At the time, I knew little about Don, only that he was somewhat of a legend in Silicon Valley for his role, many years ago, in bringing technologies like the floppy disk drive and the first low-cost hard drive to the market.

During our conversation, Don asked me if I had considered focusing more on the insider security threat. In his opinion, this was a major problem that was only getting worse. That question gave me the initial idea for the book you are now about to read. More important, Don then told me that his new company, Reconnex Corp., was doing what he called groundbreaking work in the area of identifying and stopping insider threats. When I prodded him for more information, it was immediately clear that the company was, in fact, doing something unique and critical to security.

I then arranged to tour the company and meet with its executives and engineers to learn more about their technology and what they were discovering in the course of working with government and private sector enterprises. The interviews I conducted at Reconnex revealed the first real data to demonstrate the extent of the insider threat from both a security and legal liability perspective. The data that the company amassed through its risk assessments was several orders of magnitude more detailed and of a much higher quality than any previous study (most of which have simply been surveys) of the insider threat.

This work, therefore, is the result of hundreds of hours of research and interviews with the experts at Reconnex, as well as leading authorities in the fields of counterintelligence, criminal psychology, law enforcement, and information security. The documents reviewed for this text include FBI affidavits, criminal indictments, Congressional testimonies, internal Defense Department and intelligence community studies, as well as unprecedented access to more than 50 confidential risk assessments conducted at some of the nation's largest companies and government agencies. However, at no time during the research of this book was the author granted access to the proprietary data of any of the companies or government agencies that underwent voluntary risk assessments. In addition, attempts have been made, where appropriate, to conceal the identities of the companies, agencies and individuals who cooperated with the research for this book. This was done strictly for security and privacy reasons.

This, therefore, is a faithful attempt to provide an exhaustive study of the insider threat to propriety data and America's economic competitiveness to date. It is a story that has no end, but it is a story that is all too real. Everything outlined in the following pages actually happened.

Cast Of Characters

The Storytellers

Don Massaro
Silicon Valley veteran and CEO of Reconnex Corp.

Dan Verton
Author of *Black Ice: The Invisible Threat of Cyber-Terrorism* and *The Hacker Diaries: Confessions of Teenage Hackers*

The Unknown, Suspected, Accused and Convicted

Charles Revson
Founder of REVLON

Jonathan Pollard
Former Navy Intelligence Analyst and Convicted Spy

Aldrich Hazen Ames
Former Chief, CIA Soviet Counterintelligence, and Convicted Spy

Ramon Garcia
The pseudonym of Robert Phillip Hanssen

Robert Phillip Hanssen
Former FBI Intelligence Analyst and Convicted Spy

Victor Cherkashin
Former Soviet KGB Agent

Mario Castillo
Former FBI Agent

Jeffrey D. Fudge
Former FBI Agent

Country A, B, & D
U.S. Allies Known to Spy on U.S. Corporations

iv

Dr. Wen Ho Lee
Former Los Alamos National Laboratory Scientist Accused and Acquitted of Espionage

China's Corporate Spies

Yan Ming Shan
Hai Lin
Kai Xu
Yong-Qing Cheng
Fei Ye
Ming Zhong
Junsheng Wang
Bin Wu
Pin Yen Yang
Hwei Chen Yang
Ten Hong "Victor" Lee
Hsu Kai-lo
Chester H. Ho

The Disgruntled

Thomas A. Varlotta
Former FAA IT Project Manager

Ana Belen Montes
Former DIA Cuban Intelligence Analyst

Timothy Allen Lloyd
Former System Administrator

Corporate Insiders

Philip J. Cummings
Jean Pierre "Johnny" Harper
Mark Kovack
Abdelkader Smires
David Alan Wolf
Cynthia Reynolds
Randy McArthur
Dean Johnson
Barbara Jane Coward
Gary D. Jones
Seven (7) GTE Managers
Daniel Wiant

Carol Watson
Say Lye Ow
William P. Genovese
Igor Serebryany
John Morris
William Garrison
Richard Gerhardt
Kenneth Patterson
John Sullivan
Hiroaki Serizawa
Jolene Rector
Steven Snyder

The Victims

REVLON
Hazel Bishop Cosmetics
U.S. Navy
Central Intelligence Agency
Defense Intelligence Agency
Federal Bureau of Investigation
Department of Defense
Department of Energy
Federal Aviation Administration
U.S. State Department
Acuson Corp.
3DGeo Development Inc.
Lucent Technologies Inc.
Sun Microsystems Inc.
NEC Electronics Corp.
Transmeta Corp.
Trident Microsystems Inc.
Omega Engineering Corp.
Avery Dennison Corp.
Applied Materials Inc.
Bristol-Myers Squibb
Wells Fargo Bank
Northrup Grumman
Lockheed Martin Corp.
Sumitomo Mitsui Bank
Compass Bank
First Midwest Bank
Beverly Hills Bar Association
North Island Financial Credit Union
Bank of Ephraim

Telecommunications Data Inc.
Ford Motor Credit
Brookwood Companies, Inc.
Utah Copper Employee's Credit Union
Friskies Petcare
Nestle U.S.
GTE
American Cancer Society
Watson Coatings Inc.
Varian Semiconductor Equipment Associates Inc.
Intel Corp.
Microsoft Corp.
Mainsoft Corp.
DirecTV
Jones Day Reavis & Pogue
Mphasis BPO of India
Wendt Corp.
American Eagle Outfitters
Lance Inc.
Learner Research Institute
Harvard Medical School
R.P. Scherer Inc.
Internet Trading Technologies Inc.

The Risk Assessment Players

Anonymous – Major federal agencies
Anonymous – Several large U.S. financial institutions
Anonymous – Several of the largest IT companies in the U.S.
Anonymous – A major U.S.-based manufacturing company
Anonymous — A leading company in the transportation industry
Anonymous – Several of the nation's major government and private healthcare
        providers
Anonymous – A major U.S.-based biotech company

Foreword

Open Letter to CEOs

By Don Massaro

To my fellow CEOs:

I hate to tell you this, but you have a major problem, and you have no idea how serious it is. This problem literally threatens the life of your business—its corporate secrets, shareholder value, critical infrastructure, and corporate governance. It is the security threat that starts from inside your company – what we refer to as the "Insider Threat." Even companies that have spent millions of dollars implementing the most sophisticated perimeter network security systems available are not protected from the insider threat, which accounts for more than 80 percent of all corporate security breaches today. Former Attorney General John Ashcroft estimated in October 2004 that intellectual property theft costs U.S. companies $250 billion per year. And that dollar amount does not take into account the intangible losses to competitive advantage or corporate reputation.

Both Dan Verton and I knew the insider threat existed. I started a company to address the problem; Dan wrote this book. Yet, even though the two of us knew about the problem, we had no idea how pervasive and serious it was - how threatening it was to the very life of a business - until we saw the anonymous data.

The company I co-founded in 2003, named Reconnex, has developed a content-based security appliance that analyzes all network traffic and information leaving a network, whether it's an e-mail, a posting to a webpage, a photograph, a spreadsheet, or corporate source code. The goal is to help corporations prevent the accidental or intentional disclosure of confidential or proprietary information. After reading Dan's book *Black Ice*, which delved into the threats of cyber-terrorism, I realized there was another dimension to the risks facing our corporate clients - the cyber-criminal working inside the corporation. I invited Dan to Mountain View, California, our corporate headquarters, to make a presentation to my executive staff. We were fascinated with what Dan was doing and he was fascinated with what we were doing.

Over the next year we developed a close working relationship with Dan, and he gave us a lot of insight into the mind and activities of the cyber-criminal. This insight had a significant effect on our future product planning. In particular, it became very important for us to have the ability to quickly reveal to companies what was happening inside their networks, so that they could see the business implications for themselves.

A key element of the Reconnex solution today is what we call the 48-hour e-Risk Rapid Assessment. The assessment analyzes the content flowing in and out of corporate networks and provides a detailed report pinpointing competitive vulnerabilities, productivity losses, corporate infrastructure failures, and personal and legal liability issues that could damage or disrupt a company's business, brand and/or shareholder value. The report also provides steps for the remediation of these issues.

Without exception, every company we have assessed to date is surprised to find out the extent to which they are still at risk. And as you and I know, surprises are what keep CEOs, corporate risk managers, and corporate security officers up at night.

The more 48-hour e-Risk Assessments we perform for corporate and government accounts, the more we are amazed at our findings.

Consider these examples. One company learned that an employee had sent private data about more than 200 customers to a personal Hotmail account—even though the company had outlawed Web mail usage on their network. One company had a policy requiring employees to encrypt confidential customer information, but less than 12 percent of the information sent was actually encrypted. In another case, we found more than 2000 HIPAA violations involving employee and patient data leaving a health facility's network unencrypted. Another hospital learned the names and personal information of 500 patients with AIDS, left their network and went to a Yahoo! Web mail account. One very large global company found that strategic marketing and business plans were sent to a direct competitor by a current employee. A Fortune 100 High Tech company learned proprietary technical design documents were being sent to personal e-mail accounts by employees trying to start their own business in the same industry. All of these incidents are unacceptable risks carrying the ability to disrupt or destroy a business if left undetected.

It was results like these that prompted Dan to follow up his book on cyber-terrorism with a book on the insider threat.

The fact that confidential and proprietary information is "leaking" from corporate networks should not be a surprise to most security professionals. Insider threats have existed for a very long time. But security professionals also know that virtually all of the security systems put in place over the last twenty years were designed to prevent the threat from "outside the company." Firewalls, intrusion detection/prevention systems, virus detection, authentication and authorization systems, and similar perimeter security products operate under the assumption that the "bad guys" live outside the corporate network, and folks inside the corporate network are the "good guys."

But what if the "bad guys" are inside? What if your major security leaks - the ones that had the greatest financial impact on your company – originated from the inside? Then the "guns" are pointed in the wrong direction. Actually, you need guns pointed in both directions: one set for the threat from the outside and the other set for the threat from inside. It is unfortunately a two-front war.

Fortunately, technology has evolved so that we can wage this two-front war. Until recently, we were not able to assess the extent of the problem, let alone solve it. We did not have the processing power, the capture power, or the analysis power. So the issue was more or less ignored. As a result of the recent developments of gigabit network switches and content switching devices, the necessary technologies are now available to attack the insider threat at the content level. With networks running at gigabit speeds, we can capture and index all content flowing in and out of networks in real time. And with improvements in packet-processing technologies, we have the power to parse and compare content in real time.

In this world of global interconnectedness, global competition, outsourcing, and regulatory compliance, enterprises must think beyond the perimeter to secure their corporate electronic assets. The rash of intellectual property theft cases in the news recently is a testimony to that. In the following pages, Dan takes us on a journey through some of the more interesting (and damaging) high profile cases of insider security breeches. You get a vivid picture of the "who, what, where, how and why" of these breeches and insight into the mental state of the insiders responsible. Dan also takes us through the kinds of real-life "data leakage" we are finding today with the latest in content-based monitoring technology. Finally, he explains how the technology can ultimately solve the insider threat problem for companies like yours.

I think you will find the book fascinating or upsetting, depending upon your perspective. But either way, the problem cannot be ignored. What is leaving our corporate and government networks affects the security and prosperity of this country. The good news is that we are no longer ignoring the problem. We possess the technology to fix it.

Donald J. Massaro
President & CEO
Reconnex Corporation
Mt. View, California
May 9, 2005

Introduction

This is a book about life and death in the age of information. It explores the bizarre, itinerant life of proprietary data and the death of the security perimeter. These facts of the modern corporate and government enterprise may come as a surprise to many. Most of us, after all, assume that proprietary or secret data are protected and kept under tight control. Likewise, we assume that such control stems from clearly-defined physical and electronic boundaries, within which only the authorized and trusted roam.

Think again.

Prior to the terrorist attacks against the United States on September 11, 2001, security practitioners were quick to point out that despite the increasing number of hacker, virus and worm attacks, the greatest threat to an enterprise's intellectual property originated inside the organization. Those with authorized access to data were the source of the greatest number and most costly security incidents involving intellectual property. Sometimes the incidents were the result of malicious, criminal intent – a disgruntled employee who had been passed over for promotion, or a dishonest individual who saw a quick way to earn an extra buck by selling corporate secrets to a competitor. At other times the incidents were the result of inadvertent disclosures by untrained personnel who were unaware of either the sensitivity of the information or corporate policies governing who should be granted access to the data.

Regardless of the mode of disclosure (intentional or unintentional), pre-9/11 America had it right. The insider threat was – and as you will see, still is – the biggest threat to the security and stability of the nation and the private companies that constitute its economic engine. Why? The answer to that question is simple: because information has replaced the dollar bill as the currency of the new Internet economy. Today, the modern enterprise is valued most by its intangible assets – its intellectual property. And what is meant by intellectual property? For our purposes in this book, intellectual property can mean trademarks, copyrights, patents, research and development data, software specifications, internal policies and procedures, customer and vendor data, human capital (know-how), sales and business strategies, and, of course, classified information used by government agencies for purposes of national security.

Despite the obvious value of such information, the terrorist attacks of 9/11 and the resulting phenomenon we now call the "Department of Homeland Security" shifted America's attention toward all things external and foreign. In the four years since the attacks, we have become obsessed with the external threat – that which is gathering in far-away places and attempting to transport its chaos to America's shores. And while this is certainly a legitimate national security concern — especially in the age of nuclear, biological and chemical terrorism — our dogged determination to defeat the foreign terrorist threat has distracted us from the ongoing work of the enemy within. The threat posed by the malicious insider not only remains with us, but also continues to grow in sophistication, boldness and overall economic cost. And as you will see, that cost is estimated to be in the tens of billions of dollars annually.

Ironically, the same technological development that has revolutionized the world of business is now making the act of doing business increasingly dangerous for companies of all sizes. Information technologies have evolved at such a rapid pace that their corresponding rapid insertion into corporate and government enterprises has literally obliterated the notion of the security perimeter. In the old world of paper-based communications, it was relatively easy to control the flow of information. Documents were created on typewriters, sometimes in duplicate or triplicate using carbon paper, and could then be stored in locked filing cabinets or safes. The originator of the document knew how many copies he or she had made, how many were still in existence and where they were stored. The personal computer and the Internet, however, have destroyed forever the concept of controlling information flow. Today, the modern business and government enterprise would be hard-pressed to identify the electronic boundaries that separate them from the rest of the world. In addition, those same organizations would likely find it even more difficult to identify all of the locations where their electronic assets – their digital intellectual property – reside. The reality is that most organizations, regardless of size, budget or industry, don't know where their data lives or who has access to it. The security perimeter that once provided at least a modicum of security no longer even does that much. When the history of the Internet age is written, the security perimeter will be counted among the first things to have become extinct.

This is the reality that confronts today's modern enterprise. However, it is a reality that most security practitioners and senior decision makers have yet to acknowledge. Their businesses and agencies are hemorrhaging secrets and they don't even know it. For those unfortunate enough to be awakened to the problem after the fact, their response is often simply to fire the offender(s), leaving the conditions that led to the crime in place. Such reactive approaches to security leave critical gaps in place that can then be exploited by the next unscrupulous employee or business partner who manages to evade early detection.

While the activities of malicious insiders may be difficult to detect, conducting insider crimes is only getting easier with each passing day. New technologies have lowered the bar considerably when it comes to the technological prowess required to carry out insider crimes or conduct electronic espionage. Surprisingly, very few insider crimes involve the use of sophisticated scripts or software programs. To the contrary, they often involve legitimate user activity and require little knowledge of network security. Further complicating matters is the availability of easy-to-use "ordinary" devices such as picture phones and keychain Universal Serial Bus (USB) storage devices. As a former intelligence officer in the U.S. Marine Corps, I can recall having to submit to searches each time I left the Sensitive Compartmented Information Facility (SCIF) where I worked. The security officer would look through my bags and thumb through any documents I had in my possession, searching for classified information. Today, such searches are irrelevant given the possible presence of USB storage devices that look like ordinary ink pens and key chains. Also, documents that used to take an insider multiple trips or multiple briefcases to carry now fit easily in these small storage devices. Application security is another real concern for organizations dealing with insider activity, as well as new legal requirements, such as the Sarbanes-Oxley Act of 2002 and the Gramm-Leach-Bliley Act of 1999, which outline corporate governance and personal information disclosure reporting requirements, respectively. Although the technical sophistication of a malicious or criminal insider might be relatively low, such users often gain detailed knowledge of specific application vulnerabilities, workarounds and administrative overrides that can easily facilitate insider abuse. It is also interesting to note that these and other types of insiders are often not employed in technical positions. It is no longer necessary to have a degree in computer science to steal or corrupt sensitive, classified or privacy-protected data.

The low level of technological know-how required to conduct most forms of insider abuse raises interesting questions about the psychological profile of the average malicious insider. As you will see, there are many personality traits that malicious insiders share. There may also be similarities in the circumstances surrounding the personal lives of perpetrators that may act as instigating factors in their decision to strike out at a perceived injustice. However, while recent studies have focused almost exclusively on the psychological profiles of information technology professionals (e.g. system administrators, help-desk technicians, etc.--who have the technical ability to misuse computer assets in a way that would prevent them from getting caught), it is important that we not confine our understanding of malicious insider behavior to this one group of professionals. Insiders come in all shapes and sizes, and from all educational and professional backgrounds. They can also be found in almost any division within a particular company or organization, and can often be contract employees, subcontractors, service providers or the employees of an outsourcing firm. All of these individuals are capable of not only stealing your organization's secrets, but also of putting it in potentially-catastrophic legal turmoil. Again, the security perimeter no longer exists.

The only way to combat the insider threat is to adopt a defense-in-depth security strategy that does more than simply monitor access attempts from outside the electronic enterprise. It must also monitor the flow of information from within. By its very nature, a defense-in-depth strategy has at its core an organization's most precious assets: its information and its knowledge. And that is what this book is about.

The pages that follow are the result of unprecedented access to a security company that has designed new, ground-breaking technology that is opening the eyes of all who try it to the startling amount of sensitive data leaving corporate and government networks every hour of every day. While I have provided a healthy amount of historical data and analysis to demonstrate the evolution of the insider threat, it is through an exclusive agreement with Reconnex Corp. of Mountain View, Calif., that I have been able to analyze real-world security incidents involving both malicious and inadvertent disclosures of proprietary data and other forms of insider abuse of computer assets that could have resulted in significant legal liability for the companies and government agencies involved. This access has given me the most specific cross-industry data on the insider threat to corporations and government agencies to date.

Throughout this book I have provided first-hand accounts of dozens of risk assessments. And the findings are nothing less than frightening. In the banking and finance sector, for example, a Fortune 400 financial services firm watched as the private data of 200 of its customers was communicated to a private Hotmail e-mail account. That same firm also witnessed thousands of pieces of proprietary customer data leave its network unencrypted and a potential leak of a decision to downgrade a publicly traded stock.

In the high-tech sector, executives at a Fortune 100 technology developer were shocked to learn that proprietary engineering documents were sent to a competitor. Subsequent forensic investigation revealed it was the work of an insider who was seeking a new job.

Government agencies are also hemorrhaging sensitive and privacy-protected data. And the Reconnex risk assessments conducted to date reveal a problem as big, if not bigger, than that faced by the private sector. A government healthcare organization, for example, discovered an employee had leaked military casualty reports (likely to the press). Another such healthcare institution, where the private data of senior government officials is known to be stored, confirmed more than 2,000 violations of the Health Insurance Portability and Accountability Act (HIPAA). And several other federal agencies, all of which thought they were successfully blocking access to inappropriate

Web content, were shocked when the Reconnex technology quickly uncovered thousands of pornographic images, hate and racist Web pages, and gambling Web pages.

In the private sector healthcare industry, officials at one particular hospital "had a gut feeling" that private patient data was leaking out of their enterprise. In less than 48 hours, technicians from Reconnex confirmed their worst fears; information on more than 500 patients with HIV/AIDS was pulled from a private Yahoo e-mail account.

The reader should understand, however, that I have signed a non-disclosure agreement with Reconnex Corp. in return for this unusual level of access. Although I have been able to interview the company's executives and engineers at length regarding the development of their technology and their findings during initial customer trials and risk assessments, at no time was I granted access to proprietary customer data. All of the data and statistics provided, however, are factual.

The insider threat is a problem of immense proportions and one that we are only now beginning to come to terms with. But we may not be moving fast enough. What I have found in my interviews and work with the experts at Reconnex is proof positive that many of America's largest corporations and government agencies are standing at the edge of disaster.

-- Dan Verton
Washington, D.C., 2005

PART I

THE INSIDER PROFILE

Introduction to Part I

To understand the psychology of the dangerous, high-tech insider — that is, to understand why some people steal, spy or betray their loyalty to country or employer — one must understand the nature of change in the digital world and the impact that technology has had on the workplace. Change, in this context, has not been a good thing for security or for people in general. In fact, the argument can be made that the growth of the Internet and the shift that has occurred in the way people communicate, work, play, collaborate, socialize and learn has had unintended, negative consequences on the psychological makeup of a large portion of the American workforce.

The motivations of malicious insiders are as varied as the techniques used to commit sabotage, espionage, theft or extortion. However, recent studies of the psychological profiles of malicious insiders have revealed several common characteristics that make information technology professionals (particularly system administrators) an "at risk" population for malicious insider activity. In addition, these common traits make this group more vulnerable to outside manipulation by other criminals or international espionage efforts.

The most notable study was "Inside the Mind of the Insider," conducted by Eric Shaw, a former CIA psychological profiler, and Jerrold Post, a former CIA psychologist and a noted expert on the psychology of terrorism and political violence. Post, who developed the Camp David Profiles for former President Jimmy Carter, characterizes internal cyber crime as a subset of workplace violence.

"In almost every case, the act which occurs in the information system era is the reflection of unmet personal needs that are channeled into the area of expertise," Post said in an interview I conducted with him in July 2001.

According to Post, while the majority of hackers are little more than garden-variety criminals, the world of cyber-crime does have its share of Lee Harvey Oswalds. One example is Abraham Abdallah, a 32-year-old Brooklyn busboy who in March 2001 managed to pull off the biggest Internet identity heist in history, stealing the online identities of 200 of the richest people in America. There is little difference in motivation between criminals like Abdallah and Oswald, Post said during our interview in 2001. "To steal somebody's identity is to escape from one's place of insignificance. It's a special species of assassination," he says.

Increasingly, however, identity theft is simply a means to a criminal end, usually illicit financial gain. And again, those we should be most concerned about are the very individuals we entrust with managing critical data and systems. "Almost all of these people are loyal at the time of hiring," Post said, "so this isn't a matter of screening them out."

It is, however, a matter of knowing who is at risk of malicious insider activity, how to recognize the warning signs, and how to manage and relieve workplace stressors that may push an employee over the edge.

The one common characteristic shared by most IT specialists who are at risk of taking part in malicious insider activity is introversion. This finding by Post and Shaw has been observed first-hand by the author during 15 years of intelligence, security and journalism experience. It is important to note, however, that as with all of the personality traits shared by IT workers and malicious insiders the purpose of studying their prevalence is not to make a judgment about such traits or the general population that exhibits such traits, but rather to study their occurrence in cases where insider crimes are committed. And it is in that context that introversion plays a significant role in the incidence of high-tech insider crimes.

As Post and Shaw instruct us, system administrators tend to prefer the non-personal nature of Internet communications and, as a result, often demonstrate less developed interpersonal and social skills. As such, these individuals are usually more prone to deal with conflict in a detached, unconstructive, potentially hostile manner. Flame e-mails are sent to co-workers and superiors; face-to-face discussions, when they do occur, are usually focused solely on personal gripes about how poorly the workplace is being managed, the illogical decisions that others are making regarding IT systems and networks, and how only select employees (primarily the individual doing the complaining) are underappreciated and overworked by senior managers. However, while many honest individuals share similar feelings and personality traits, the malicious insider often experiences a breaking point. That breaking point, as we've already seen in the cases of Aldrich Ames and other high-profile insiders, can stem from the confluence of work stressors that go unaddressed by managers and personal conflicts, such as divorce, alcoholism, financial problems and a vast array of other stressful family matters.

The particular type of introvert we are talking about here also often demonstrates a high level of computer dependency. This is not surprising given the current research on general hacker activity. Those individuals who become malicious computer hackers often display an unhealthy dependence on computer communications and friendships and, as a result, develop a disdain for others outside of their Internet-based social circles. Likewise, the independent nature of living an Internet life (as opposed to nurturing one's social skills in the real world) often creates individuals who do not function well in a team environment. The real world, where senior managers and government decision makers live and work, does not allow one to simply disconnect' or find an alternate chat room where one's opinions and beliefs are more widely shared and supported.

It is worth noting, however, that the author found many examples of traditional teenage hackers who, in addition to demonstrating a high degree of computer dependence, also lived highly social lives outside of the Internet realm. So this characterization, as mentioned earlier, must be considered on a case by case basis. Yet, the common traits shared by most known malicious insiders can be observed first-hand at any of the annual Black Hat or DefCon conferences, both of which are held each year in Las Vegas and attract self-proclaimed "hackers" who are often gainfully employed in the security industry. Within this subgroup one can find an even smaller subgroup of individuals who act out maliciously in their electronic worlds as a means of compensating for their own sense of inadequacy. Of course, while the vast majority of information technology professionals and those who attend these conferences are honest, loyal employees, there is a subgroup of individuals who clearly demonstrate the type of character traits that managers need to be aware of — particularly disdain for authority and what Post and Shaw call "ethical flexibility."

A study of malicious insiders, conducted in 1990 and 1993, concluded that members of the hacker community who expressed high levels of dissatisfaction with the status quo and who made a conscious choice to alienate themselves from the non-Internet world suffered from "revenge syndrome." These individuals are often difficult to manage, feel that they know better than their supervisors, and usually attempt to infect the rest of the workforce with feelings of disdain for management decisions. These frustrations in the workplace are also usually accompanied by similar frustrations in private life. And if one were able to look into the history of these individuals (within the confines of the law, of course), a pattern of problems dealing with authority and family conflict would likely emerge.

The issue of ethical flexibility is an interesting phenomenon that is highly relevant to the world of IT. There are countless examples, including those made public through legal proceedings and those known to the author on a non-disclosure basis, where system administrators have acknowledged quasi-ownership of the organization's IT systems and network. This often results when the IT administrator feels that he or she has done all of the work required to keep the system running properly only to have policies or initiatives countermanded by business managers with less knowledge and sympathy for the IT department. In extreme cases, these individuals can lash out at the organization (e.g. sabotage, malingering, theft, etc...) because they feel entitled to a certain kind of treatment and believe wrongly that their actions, regardless of how malicious, are justified given the situation. This is what the author would call the "I'll show them" syndrome, in which an employee endeavors to prove their worth (including the validity of their opinions and the implications of what they consider a misappropriation of their time and skill) by manufacturing a crisis — a crisis that results either from a direct action on the part of the employee or a crisis that stems from an act of omission (not doing something, such as installing a software patch, that he/she knows will lead to a security incident). Those with a flexible sense of right and wrong, however, consider their actions justified given the situation.

In another study conducted by S.J. Harrington[1] in 1995, many such individuals were characterized as lacking the moral inhibitions that prevent the majority of people from taking such actions. In fact, Harrington went as far as to conclude that his data indicates as many as 7% of IT professionals do not object to hacking, cracking, espionage or sabotage. This is precisely the mindset of a large subgroup of individuals who attend the Black Hat and DefCon conferences each year. They believe fervently that any and all computers or networks that operate with open security flaws are fair game for hacking. Many of these individuals even believe such systems should be hacked to teach the operators a public lesson and, in their twisted logic, shame organizations into improving security and the quality of software.

Chapter 1

The Old Breed

"I don't think if the competition have got [sic] something wonderful, whomever they may be, that there is anything wrong in looking at it, and copying it."
-- Charles Revson, founder of Revlon.[2]

C harles Revson would have made a fine director of Central Intelligence. After all, the founder of the renowned cosmetics company Revlon was obsessed with keeping his closely-held secrets out of the hands of his competition (Elizabeth Arden, Estee Lauder, Max Factor and just about anybody who endeavored to make a living in the market that Revson felt belonged to him and him alone). He was also semi-obsessed with "adopting" others' secrets to dominate the cosmetics industry.

Revson took no shortcuts. He assigned all of his products code names and spoke about them in the vaguest manner possible. He instituted CIA-like information controls, including a strict internal need-to-know policy for product ingredients. While relaxing aboard his lavish yacht, Revson was ever mindful of what clandestine CIA operatives refer to as COMSEC – communications security. He feared the likes of Max Factor and others would employ sophisticated listening devices to tap into his onboard radio communications. Revson, after all, had something to protect.

Revson founded the company in 1932, along with his brother Joseph and a chemist named Charles Lachman, who contributed the "L" in the Revlon name. Starting with a single product – nail enamel that was considered truly distinctive in the industry– the three founders developed a unique manufacturing process. Using pigments instead of dyes, Revlon was able to offer a luxuriant-looking, opaque nail enamel in a wide variety of shades that until then had been unavailable. In only six years, Revson and his partners turned the company into a multimillion-dollar organization, launching what was to become one of the most recognized cosmetics names in the world.

Surprisingly, however, Revson's paranoia and the extreme measures he took to protect his cosmetics enterprise from prying eyes wasn't enough to stop a memo containing the secret names of each item in one of his future hypoallergenic product lines (code named New Jersey) from being leaked to his arch rivals.[3]

One can imagine Revson's reaction when he saw an advertisement for Estee Lauder's Clinique cosmetics line in *Women's Wear Daily* that exposed every product name contained in the Revlon memo. Revson was livid. He immediately mandated that all employees sign in and out of the office and issued ID cards to all. But Revson wasn't satisfied with taking a defensive posture. There was something to be said for intelligence collection as well.

In the 1950s, Hazel Bishop cosmetics owner Raymond Spector became increasingly suspicious after Revlon began beating him to market with what Spector thought were his secret ideas. He was convinced that Revson was listening to his private communications. He then conducted a private disinformation campaign to see if false information would also be divulged. It was. Spector then hired two wiretapping experts, who quickly discovered that his telephones and office had been compromised by listening devices. Spector was convinced Revson was behind the electronic eavesdropping.[4]

In 1955, Bill Heller, one of Revson's closest confidants and the eventual secretary/treasurer and director of international operations at Revlon, testified before the New York State Wiretap hearings that for five or six years Revlon, with the help of its local telephone service provider, had been monitoring conversations of certain of its employees to be sure they were handling customer service calls properly. Heller also testified that on one occasion he arranged to have a detective agency install a tape recorder in a locked closet that would automatically record the conversations of a certain Revlon executive without his knowledge.[5]

Sometime in 1967, Revlon's then president, Dan Rodgers, reported hearing clicking sounds on his telephone. The telephone company soon discovered that the clicking sounds were from an unauthorized wiretap. Technicians from the telephone company, working under the watchful eye of an assistant district attorney, then traced the tap from Rodger's telephone to the office of Bill Tracy, Revlon's security chief. Upon inspecting Tracy's office, the technicians discovered a small hole and some wood shavings near the back of a credenza. According to Revson biographer Andrew Tobias, however, no wires or recording equipment were discovered. "Tracy explained to the grand jury that he had made the hole to plug in a radio so he could listen to the World Series," according to Tobias. "Witnesses claimed to have seen Tracy puttering around down in the basement; but Tracy explained that he was merely doing that in his capacity as security officer, checking to see that Revlon's lines weren't tapped."[6]

Writing in his Revson biography, *Fire and Ice: The Story of Charles Revson - the Man Who Built the Revlon Empire,* Tobias concludes that there is no way to know exactly how much internal spying took place at Revlon. But some things are certain, he said. "Bugging rumors ran rife, and when the company moved out of 666 Fifth Avenue, a network of wires was discovered in the walls -- installed, the story ran, for an intercom system that was never hooked up."[7]

.. -. ... .. -.. . / .--- --- -...

The early days of the Revlon Empire offer a good example of how pre-information age technologies could open up even the most paranoid of organizations to unintended security breeches. But that was the era before the personal computer and, more important, networked computers. Access, therefore, was still defined by penetrating the physical perimeter of the organization. To tap a telephone you needed physical access and you had to run wires. Likewise, physical access to an office was necessary to plant a listening device.

But the spying activities at Revlon would not be the last chapter in technology's storied history of unintended consequences. In fact, things were only just beginning to get interesting.

In 1960, for example, Henry Cabot Lodge, the U.S. Ambassador to the United Nations, exposed to the world the now infamous Soviet "Great Seal" bug – a primitive, but successful, example of overcoming the physical access requirement of electronic eavesdropping. The incident stemmed from a gift given by the Soviets to the U.S. Ambassador in Moscow. It was a wooden, hand-carved replica of the Great Seal of the United States, which the American ambassador hung proudly on the wall behind his desk. But hidden in the seal was a pencil-sized device equipped with a flexible diaphragm that vibrated when sound struck it. There were no wires or batteries. Instead, the Soviets parked a van outside the U.S. embassy and pointed an ultra-high frequency signal toward the bug, which was then modulated by the sounds of conversations being picked up by the bug and beamed back to the van.[8]

All of these early examples of electronic eavesdropping stem from the invention of the printed circuit and the transistor -- the nexus of which produced the electronic universe's big bang in miniaturization. Technology's inexorable march forward meant one thing: greater capability in smaller form. It was and still is an unavoidable outcome of the information technology revolution.

By 1966, for example, Life Magazine began reporting on the existence of miniature listening devices small enough to be disguised as olives in martini glasses.[9] For $500, would-be spies could purchase the plastic olive, which contained a transmitter and used a fake toothpick as an antenna. Eventually, technology provided the world of espionage with the ability to turn ordinary electrical outlets into listening devices capable of transmitting their intercepts across power lines.

But there was little that lawmakers could do at the time to stem the tide of intrusive technologies. After all, the components necessary to create many of these basic listening devices could be harvested from any transistor radio. This is the essence of what is meant by 'the unintended consequences of technology.' But soon, the arrival of the computer and of networks would remove one of the main obstacles to penetrating an organization's security perimeter: access control.

.. -. ... .. -.. . / .--- --- -...

By the late 1970s, the world in which the analog telephone had been the primary communications tool was quickly passing into oblivion, thanks to the introduction of the personal computer. Information now lived in digital format and it could roam freely. Again, the Big Bang theory applies. The combination of the written word with the personal computer produced an explosion of information. Single bits of data could now live multiple, independent lives in multiple, independent locations. And controlling the replication and spread of those bits of data became virtually impossible. For those with trusted access to information of value to the world of intelligence (competitive business intelligence or international espionage), this was a gift of unfathomable importance.

It was at this time that a young undergraduate at Stanford University began lying to his friends that he had close acquaintances within Mossad, the Israeli intelligence service. He then entered law school at Tufts University, but soon dropped out to act upon his boyhood desire to be a spy. His name was Jonathan Jay Pollard. And in 1979, he became a civilian intelligence analyst for the U.S. Navy.

By 1984, Pollard was working in the Anti-Terrorism Alert Center at the Naval Criminal Investigative Service (NCIS). There, he had access to computer databases, CIA field reports and satellite reconnaissance photographs. All published accounts to date paint a picture of Pollard as a troubled individual who suddenly and somewhat surprisingly found himself with access to some of the most sensitive and highly classified national security information in the Defense Department. Unfortunately, security officials failed to pick up on his unusual behavior and alleged personal problems.[10]

Pollard soon befriended Avi Sella, an Israeli intelligence agent who had been posing as a graduate student at New York University. Sella quickly realized that Pollard was ripe for recruiting, and asked him for any classified information he could get access to. Sella also told Pollard he would be paid handsomely. And he was.

Pollard's espionage activity involved little more than printing out reams of classified documents from his computer, placing them in a brief case, and walking out of the office. The first time he did it, Pollard walked out with classified documents detailing Iraqi chemical warfare plants. For this he received $10,000 in cash and a $10,000 diamond and sapphire ring.

His espionage activities were surprisingly monotonous. By his own admission, Pollard handed the Israeli intelligence service nearly 800 highly classified publications and more than a thousand intelligence cables from agents in the field.

However, Pollard's short, unexceptional life as a spy came to an end on November 18, 1985, when he was arrested walking out of his office holding a briefcase full of top secret documents. It was only at that point – six years after he had begun abusing his access to classified data – that Pollard's supervisors became suspicious of his insatiable appetite for classified information.

More than a decade after Pollard's arrest and sentencing to life in prison, Joseph Digenova, the U.S. Attorney who prosecuted him, told the press that authorities believed there was another person inside the intelligence community who helped Pollard. But while investigators had their suspicions about who the person could have been, they could prove nothing.

"That has always been believed because Mr. Pollard was given the numbers, the highly classified intelligence numbers of specific documents to get," Digenova said. "And no one would have known those numbers unless they had initial access to them. So it is clear there was another person in the espionage ring who was helping Mr. Pollard's Israeli handlers. That we are sure of."[11]

.. -. ... .. -.. . / .--- --- -...

When put in the context of the damage it caused to national security, Pollard's espionage is astounding in its simplicity. He was granted access to information with little or no control or boundaries, and nobody monitored or questioned his information viewing or printing habits. But what if Pollard had been a more senior official, and a spy capable of divulging the identities of covert intelligence agents working overseas on behalf of the United States, or massive electronic eavesdropping operations targeting the Soviet Union?

That's exactly what began happening shortly after Pollard was arrested and put in jail. It was the beginning of what would eventually become known as Operation Nightmover, the FBI's epic hunt for a mole inside the CIA.

The CIA first became concerned about a mole operating inside the agency in 1985, when U.S. agents recruited two Soviet embassy employees in Washington and turned them into double agents. However, Soviet officials soon recalled both agents to Moscow, where they were summarily executed. It was a devastating blow for the CIA and triggered an immediate investigation into the likely causes.

The investigation went nowhere for the next six years, even as three additional double agents based in Washington, D.C., disappeared without explanation. Then, in 1991, as the FBI officially launched Nightmover and began piecing together the movements and personal lives of everyone who had access to information pertaining to the betrayed agents, the mole hunters developed a list of 29 potential suspects. Among them was the name Aldrich Hazen Ames, the chief of the CIA's Soviet Counterintelligence Division.

Ames began his full-time career at the CIA in 1962 as a low-level clerk/typist. For the next five years, he served as a document analyst in the CIA's Directorate of Operations while attending George Washington University on a part-time basis. He graduated from GWU in the fall of 1967, by which time he had attained the grade of GS-7 and applied for the CIA's Career Training Program – the schooling required for all CIA case officers.

The CIA's initial psychological profile of Ames placed him at the low end of the spectrum in terms of the qualities the agency looked for in a case officer (those responsible for recruiting and managing foreign nationals to spy on behalf of the U.S.). Ames was considered an intellectual and a loner – two qualities that we will see again as we continue our study of insiders. Nonetheless, Ames made the cut and was sent out into the field.

Ames' first overseas tour as a case officer took him to Ankara, Turkey. There, his superiors rated his initial performance as "satisfactory." But their assessment of Ames' capabilities would quickly change. By his third year in the field, agency officials informed headquarters that Ames was not suited for fieldwork and that he should return to Langley, Virginia, for reassignment. Ames was devastated and considered leaving the CIA.[12]

Upon returning to headquarters in 1972, however, he was reassigned to the Soviet-East European Division and underwent Russian language training. His performance appraisals improved dramatically "apparently because he was more proficient in managing paperwork and planning field operations than being 'on the front lines'."[13]

Despite this temporary improvement in performance, Ames' personal and professional lives remained in a constant state of semi-controlled chaos for the next 12 years. A strained marriage and a drinking problem threatened his CIA career at almost every turn. Then, by 1984, his marriage had ended (as a new relationship with a foreign national who would become his second wife was beginning). But of greater concern to Ames were the terms of the divorce settlement, which, in his mind, threatened to bankrupt him. The following is Ames' own recollection of the financial pressure that led him to consider espionage.

> I felt a great deal of financial pressure, which, in retrospect, I was clearly overreacting to. The previous two years that I had spent in Washington, I had incurred a certain amount of personal debt in terms of buying furniture for an apartment and my divorce settlement had left me with no property essentially. Together with a cash settlement of about $12,000 to buy out my pension over time, I think I may have had about $10,000 or $13,000 in debt. It was not a

truly desperate situation but it was one that somehow really placed a great deal of pressure on me. Rosario was living with me at the time...I was contemplating the future. I had no house, and we had strong plans to have a family, and so I was thinking in the longer term.[14]

April 16, 1985 was a typical spring day in Washington, D.C.; the temperature was in the mid-50s, the skies were partly sunny and a light breeze energized the senses. It was on that day that Ames walked into the Soviet embassy in Washington and handed the duty clerk an envelope addressed to the most senior KGB agent present. Inside was a note detailing the identities of two Soviet double agents, a page from an internal CIA directory with his real name highlighted, and a request for a cash payment of $50,000. A few days later, he met face-to-face with his Soviet handler and received the cash.

According to Ames, this one-time con game[15] was planned as a means to dig himself out of his financial troubles. But this raises an obvious question: why did he continue his espionage activities? Surprisingly, nobody, not even Ames, knows for sure. In the following statement taken after he was arrested, Ames recounts what was going through his mind at the time.

> I'm still puzzled as to what took me to the next steps. The main factor, on balance I think, was a realization after I had received the $50,000, was a sense of the enormity of what I had done. I think I had managed under the stress of money and thinking, conceiving the plan I had carried out in April, I saw it as perhaps a clever, ...not a game, but a very clever plan to do one thing. ...(I)t came home to me, after the middle of May, the enormity of what I had done. The fear that I had crossed a line, which I had not clearly considered before. That I crossed a line I could never step back.[16]

And step back he did not. Without prompting from his KGB handlers, Ames then printed out "five to seven pounds" worth of top-secret documents detailing high-level spies working for the U.S., wrapped the documents in plastic and walked out of CIA headquarters.

Throughout 1986, the CIA continued to learn of one compromised source after another. It is interesting to note, however, that this was the only reason that the agency knew it had an insider problem or that highly sensitive information was leaving the confines of its headquarters facility.

As with the Pollard case, there seems to have been little control or monitoring of information access, download and printing within the CIA's counterintelligence operations during the period of Ames' spying. In fact, when detailed to Rome in July 1986, Ames routinely walked out of his office carrying shopping bags full of classified documents to pass to his Soviet counterparts. Aside from such blatant acts of espionage, there were other, less obvious clues to Ames' activities that went unnoticed. For example, former colleagues testified after his arrest that he had routinely expressed interest in intelligence matters and cases that were clearly unrelated to his current or past responsibilities. When challenged about his inquisitiveness, Ames simply said he was trying to stay abreast of intelligence matters.

On June 25, 1993, the FBI searched Ames's office at CIA headquarters and discovered 144 classified documents, most of which did not relate to his official duties. Investigators also retrieved a treasure trove of information about his activities that he had stored on his home computer. Among the documents discovered on his personal computer was a note written to his Soviet contacts, which stated, in part:

> My most immediate need, as I pointed out in March, is money. As I have mentioned several times, I do my best to invest a good part of the cash I received, but keep part of it out for ordinary expenses. Now I am faced with the need to cash in investments to meet current needs a very tight and unpleasant situation! I have had to sell a certificate of deposit in Zurich and some stock here to help make up the gap. Therefore, I will need as much cash delivered in Pipe [document drop site] as you think can be accommodated [sic] - - it seems to me that it could accommodate [sic] up to $100,000.[17]

In its report on the Ames case, the Senate Select Committee on Intelligence concluded that a major enabling factor in Ames' espionage activities was the lack of access and document control inside the CIA.

> Ames was able--without detection--to walk out of CIA headquarters and the U.S. Embassy in Rome with bags and envelopes stuffed with classified documents and materials. Many of the classified documents he passed to his KGB handlers were copies of documents that were not under any system of accountability. Ames did not even have to make copies of them. In his last job in the Counternarcotics Center at the CIA, Ames was able to "download" a variety of classified documents onto computer discs and then simply remove them to his home. When he attended a conference in Turkey in 1993, he brought a laptop computer to do work in his hotel room. This apparently raised no security concern among those familiar with the incident. He was also able to visit offices he had no reason to be in, and gain access to information he had no business seeing.

As a result, the Senate recommended that the Director of Central Intelligence "institute computer security measures to prevent employees from being able to download classified information onto computer diskettes and removing them from CIA facilities." The report also called upon the CIA to reevaluate its policies governing the "introduction, accountability, dissemination, removal, and destruction of all forms of electronic media" and to upgrade its "ability...to audit specific computer-related functions in order to detect and monitor the actions of suspected offenders."

By the time of his arrest on February 21, 1994, Aldrich Ames had betrayed more than 100 covert intelligence gathering operations and more than three dozen covert operatives working on behalf of the United States and its allies. And as with Pollard, a simple capability to monitor access, download and printing of electronic files could have helped stop the hemorrhaging of classified information years earlier.

.. -. ... .. -.. . / .--- --- -...

The examples of Jonathan Pollard and Aldrich Ames are instructive in what they teach us about the underlying human factors that contribute to disloyalty, particularly disloyalty at the level of betraying one's own country. In fact, Pollard and Ames meet the requirements of all four pre-conditions for insider betrayal identified by Defense Department researchers in 2000.[18]

First, both had an opportunity to commit their crimes. For Pollard, the opportunity came in the form of access to intelligence databases that contained information he had little or no "need-to-know." Likewise, Pollard does not seem to have been concerned about any difficulties or dangers surrounding his access. His supervisors failed to monitor his work habits and nobody searched the bags he used to carry classified documents. As for Ames, opportunity came as a result of his senior, trusted position with the CIA and the fact that he had to know many of the secrets he eventually disclosed to do his job. However, he too showed little or no concern that his electronic viewing or printing habits would be questioned.

Second, both demonstrated an ability to "overcome natural inhibitions to criminal behavior, such as moral values, loyalty to employer or co-workers, or fear of being caught."[19] This is, perhaps, the most interesting aspect of the insider threat, especially since many people have the opportunity as well as the financial and personal motives that might make betrayal an option and yet very few cross that fateful line. In fact, the Defense Department's study of insider espionage cases tells us "moral values, loyalty and fear are the bedrock on which security is built."[20] It is because of these factors that betrayal in the national security realm is actually a rare occurrence, according to the Defense Department study.

Third, both Pollard and Ames experienced a "trigger"[21] that set their betrayal in motion. Triggers can come in almost any form and from any source of stress. For example, emotional problems, marital and financial difficulties, substance abuse and failure to compete with peers or deal with perceived injustices at work can all be triggers that push a person beyond their ability to cope with the stress.

Finally, Pollard and Ames both exhibited "a need to be satisfied" through their crimes. Pollard, for example, exhibited a need to bolster his sense of self-importance. This is evident in his alleged life-long desire to be a spy and to live a life that was much more significant and sexy than his real life actually was. Ames, on the other hand, may have concealed his deeper emotional needs under the guise of needing to make a quick buck. Money, after all, is valued for more than its ability to stop creditors from calling. Money is also about power and influence. And for lackluster performer Ames, the need to be perceived as somebody with power and influence can be seen in what he did with the hundreds of thousands of dollars he received from the Soviets (later Russia): he paid cash for a $540,000 home; he bought two Jaguar automobiles; he also ran up $455,000 in credit card bills, paid for his wife's college tuition, purchased condominiums in Bogata and Cartegena, Columbia (his second wife's native country), and invested heavily in the stock market. Ames did all of this on a CIA salary of less than $70,000 a year.

.. -. ... .. -.. . / .--- --- -...

As the details of the Pollard and Ames insider espionage cases fade from our collective memory, we are faced with a new post-Cold War world and an ever-increasing array of potential threats. The government, with its file cabinets, safes and text-based electronic databases full of national security secrets, is no longer the sole target of foreign intelligence agencies or disgruntled or troubled insiders. Today, America derives its economic and military power from the private sector, which is largely responsible for the information age revolution. And as a result, the focus of the nation's enemies has shifted.

However, a troubling confluence of circumstances has accompanied that shift. America's workers continue to be downsized, right sized and outsourced overseas, resulting in lost jobs, lower wages, fewer benefits, lower quality of life and a skilled workforce that feels nervous and without a champion in Washington, D.C. This has resulted in tens of thousands of families living paycheck-to-paycheck and workers feeling little or no loyalty to their current employer.

When combined with the breakneck pace of technology development, which has made access to proprietary information easier to obtain and conceal, and the increasing economic stress that many technology workers are dealing with today, it is not unreasonable to foresee a period of increased malicious and opportunistic insider activity throughout the government and the private sector. A new breed of insider has almost surely been born in America. Now, we must learn what those insiders are doing, how they are doing it, and how to stop them.

News Story

Cisco looking into source-code leak

An estimated 800MB of code may have been stolen

News Story by Scarlet Pruitt

MAY 17, 2004 (IDG NEWS SERVICE) - Cisco Systems Inc. is investigating the possible theft of proprietary source code that drives its networking hardware, a company representative confirmed today.

Russian security site SecurityLab.ru reported Saturday that the operating system code -- used to power a majority of the company's networking devices -- was stolen from Cisco's corporate network, with some leaked onto the Internet.

The site estimated that around 800MB of code was taken. "Cisco is aware that a potential compromise of proprietary information has occurred and was reported on a public Web site right before the weekend," Cisco spokesman Marc Musgrove said today. "The Cisco security team is looking into this matter and investigating what happened."

Musgrove declined to confirm how much of the company's code may have been stolen.
Since the leak has not yet been verified, it could turn out to be a hoax, said Chris Paget, senior security adviser at Next Generation Security Software Ltd. He pointed out that few people could actually identify the code.

However, if the code has been leaked, there is a potential for problems, since it affects most of Cisco's current, major equipment, Paget said.

The incident would mark the second time in recent months that a major vendor's source code has been leaked to the public. In February, code underlying Microsoft Corp.'s Windows NT and Windows 2000 operating systems was made available on the Internet. However, that breach didn't lead to any serious security threats.

Chapter 2

The New Breed

"You might as well sell this to us. We are going to get it anyway."
– FBI records quoting the U.S. representative of a firm brokering
technology transfer to a major foreign power.[22]

The fall of the Soviet Union and the end of the Cold War had a profound impact not only on how security and intelligence professionals viewed the world of espionage but also on the motivations of the players and the targets of their espionage activities. Global rivalries centered on technology development and intellectual capital replaced the old divides of East versus West and Communism versus Capitalism as the primary driver of the new espionage. And the new espionage widened the playing field to include private companies and corporate spies. Suddenly, the front lines of confrontation ran through corporate America instead of Western Europe and the periphery of the Far East. Thus, the captains of industry replaced four-star military commanders as the architects of the new battlefield. And America's counterintelligence experts were forced to shift their focus from ideologically motivated moles and insiders bent on betraying the nation's intelligence secrets to those who were seeking financial gain, revenge or a competitive business advantage on behalf of companies based in their native country.

Such was the beginning of the modern era of economic and industrial espionage, a time when former friends and allies suddenly became fierce economic competitors. This new reality was reflected in the language used by lawmakers in 1994 to discuss the U.S. Intelligence Authorization Act, which authorized the use of funds for fiscal year 1995. And for many, like Sen. John Warner (R-Va.), the threat of economic espionage hung over corporate America and the government like a dark cloud. The cases of economic espionage abound, said Warner.

A South Korean computer company penetrates an American competitor with a mole who plants a bug in the United States company's fax machine. A Japanese company recruits an American executive with a drug habit to support, buying sensitive bidding information and other commercial secrets. Maintenance workers walk into a U.S. company's office overseas and reprogram the telephone switching equipment to enable outsiders to eavesdrop on the company's phone calls. An American scientist goes from lab coat to turncoat, selling foreign pharmaceutical companies trade secrets that had cost $750 million in research and development costs to acquire. While much industrial espionage is solely the work of private firms, in many cases foreign governments assist or even direct economic spying activities.[23]

This was a shocking wake-up call for much of corporate America. Many business executives, for the first time, finally began to accept the truth about the world in which they did business. The death of the Soviet Union had forced the intelligence services of dozens of nations to focus on a different, non-military target. Power in the world was no longer measured by the number of tanks, ships and aircraft a nation's military had but in the technology and ingenuity that went into building those assets, which could also be spun-off into products and applications for commercial use.

Chief among the nations that threw the entire weight of its national intelligence capability behind its private industry was France. "French intelligence has long engaged in a large-scale industrial espionage program, penetrating foreign businesses, intercepting their telecommunications, and conducting a reported 10 to 15 break-ins each day at Parisian hotels to copy documents business people have left in their rooms," said Warner. "The information acquired is passed on to French industry. The governments of Japan, Germany, Belgium, the Netherlands, and other allies, as well as such countries as China are also reported to spy on behalf of their countries' industry."[24]

By 1996, government and private-sector security experts were openly supporting Congress in its effort to pass the Economic Espionage Act of that year. During a hearing of the Senate Select Committee on Intelligence (SSCI), held on Feb. 28, 1996, David E. Cooper, the then Associate Director for Defense Acquisitions Issues at the Government Accounting Office's (GAO) National Security and International Affairs Division, revealed the unclassified results of a GAO study into the economic espionage activities of several foreign governments long considered close allies of the U.S. Outlined below, "Country A" is widely believed to be France.

According to a U.S. intelligence agency, the government of Country A conducts the most aggressive espionage operation against the United States of any U.S. ally. Classified military information and sensitive military technologies are high-priority targets for the intelligence agencies of this country. Country A seeks this information for three reasons: (1) to help the technological development of its own defense industrial base, (2) to sell or trade the information with other countries for economic reasons, and (3) to sell or trade the information with other countries to develop political alliances and alternative sources of arms. According to a classified 1994 report produced by a U.S. government interagency working group on U.S. critical technology companies, Country A routinely resorts to state-sponsored espionage using covert collection techniques to obtain sensitive U.S. economic information and technology. Agents of Country A collect a variety of classified and proprietary information through observation, elicitation, and theft.[25]

Cooper also outlined the following information collection examples[26], which were provided to him by U.S. intelligence agencies:

1. An espionage operation run by the intelligence organization responsible for collecting scientific and technological information for Country A paid a U.S. government employee to obtain U.S. classified military intelligence documents.

2. Several citizens of Country A were caught in the United States stealing sensitive technology used in manufacturing artillery gun tubes.

3. Intelligence agents of Country A allegedly stole design plans for a classified reconnaissance system from a U.S. company and gave them to a defense contractor from Country A.

4. A company from Country A is suspected of surreptitiously monitoring a DOD telecommunications system to obtain classified information for Country A intelligence.

5. Citizens of Country A were investigated for allegations of passing advanced aerospace design technology to unauthorized scientists and researchers.

6. Country A is suspected of targeting U.S. avionics, missile telemetry and testing data, and aircraft communication systems for intelligence operations.

7. It has been determined that Country A targeted specialized software that is used to store data in friendly aircraft warning systems.

8. Country A has targeted information on advanced materials and coatings for collection. A Country A government agency allegedly

obtained information regarding a chemical
finish used on missile reentry vehicles from a
U.S. person.

The impact of information technologies on the international arms market
has been a major factor in the increase of insider espionage activities aimed at
U.S. software firms engaged in designing software for use in military systems.
So while the overall target of industrial espionage activities remains the U.S.
military industrial base, the definition of what organizations constitute that
base has broadened to include many hi-tech firms whose products have dual-
use military and private sector applications. This is clear from the espionage
activities orchestrated by "Country B" – another close U.S. ally (likely Germany) that U.S. intelligence analysts believe has been actively seeking to steal
U.S. technology as a means to compete with the U.S. in the global arms market.

The GAO provided the SSCI the following examples[27] of Country B's espionage efforts as documented by the U.S. intelligence community.

1. In the late 1980s, Country B's intelligence
    agency recruited agents at the European of-
    fices of three U.S. computer and electronics
    firms. The agents apparently were stealing
    unusually sensitive technical information for
    a struggling Country B company. This Coun-
    try B company also owns a U.S. company
    performing classified contracts for DOD.
2. Country B companies and government offi-
    cials have been investigated for suspected
    efforts to acquire advanced abrasive technol-
    ogy and stealth-related coatings.
3. Country B representatives have been investi-
    gated for targeting software that performs
    high-speed, real-time computational analysis
    that can be used in a missile attack system.
    Information was obtained that Country B tar-
    geted a number of U.S. defense companies
    and their missile and satellite technologies
    for espionage efforts.
4. Companies of Country B have made efforts,
    some successful, to acquire targeted compa-
    nies.

However, perhaps the most interesting of the list of foreign countries and
former allies that almost immediately began targeting U.S. technology firms
in the aftermath of the Cold War is that of "Country D." A nation with no of-

ficial intelligence service, Country D allegedly relied upon its private companies and the citizens who worked for those companies to act as its official intelligence gathering arm. And in 1996, these firms were considered to be "quite successful" in their attempts to exploit employees of U.S. companies and government agencies who had access to classified or proprietary information. According to the GAO report:

1. Firms from Country D have been investigated for targeting advanced propulsion technologies, from slush-hydrogen fuel to torpedo target motors, and attempting to export these items through intermediaries and specialty shipping companies in violation of export restrictions.
2. Individuals from Country D have been investigated for allegedly passing advanced aerospace design technology to unauthorized scientists and researchers.
3. Electronics firms from Country D directed information-gathering efforts at competing U.S. firms in order to increase the market share of Country D in the semiconductor field.[28]

In Feb. 2004, the office of the National Counterintelligence Executive (NCIX) released the ninth Annual Report to Congress on Foreign Economic Collection and Industrial Espionage. The report covered the period from January 2002 through Sept. 2003. And what it found was not surprising. Not only have a handful of major foreign powers continued the practice of employing their national intelligence services to steal U.S. trade secrets, but the growth of the Internet and increasing global tensions involving the United States have led to a substantial increase in economic espionage.[29]

According to the report, which relied upon counterintelligence databases from across the U.S. intelligence community, foreign businessmen, scientists, academics, and government officials from more than 90 countries continued targeting sensitive U.S. technologies and corporate trade secrets throughout 2003. And while it is nearly impossible to quantify the value of the data stolen, the NCIX concluded that the continued theft of military critical technologies that have dual uses in the private sector (particularly information technologies) "has eroded the U.S. global military and economic advantage and has weakened the ability of U.S. intelligence agencies to provide timely and accurate information to policymakers."[30]

Many of the espionage attempts involved overt requests for information via e-mail, fax or telephone. However, foreign governments, sometimes using hired middlemen, employed a broad array of techniques, including:

1. Acquiring or forming joint ventures with U.S. firms in order to cloud the issue of ownership.
2. Marketing foreign services and products to U.S. high-tech firms as a means of gaining access to sensitive facilities and information technology networks.
3. Using cyber-attack tools to steal sensitive U.S. information and technology or to disrupt the operations of U.S.-based competitors.
4. Sending officials, businessmen, and technical specialists to the U.S. to gather information.
5. Attending academic and scientific conferences and trade shows to target unwitting U.S. scientists, who often underestimate the importance of the information they share.
6. Applying variations of the traditional espionage techniques of spotting, assessing, and recruiting.[31]

Although all 18 of the so-called "militarily critical technologies" are routinely targeted by foreign intelligence operatives, it is the dual-use technologies (technologies that have both military and commercial applications) that remain at the top of the most wanted list. Not surprisingly, the vast majority of these dual-use technologies are not classified systems. Other predominantly civilian technologies that are routinely targeted for theft include pharmaceuticals, biometrics, nanotechnology (miniaturization), manufacturing processes, and public safety systems.

In 2000, the Defense Department reported that information systems was the most widely-sought militarily critical technology category, as it was in 1999. As many as 33 of the 63 countries associated with suspicious collection activity directly targeted information pertaining to IT systems – more than a 100% increase compared to 1999. To better understand this statistic it is important to note that the majority of defense technologies targeted that year were components rather than complete systems. This is not unusual given that IT systems are now an integral part of most major weapon systems.

Foreign intelligence operatives demonstrated the most interest in modeling and simulation technology, military radios, information security encryption devices, intrusion detection technology, satellite communications equipment and signal processing components. Likewise, transmission systems, including equipment and components used to transfer voice and data showed the greatest increase in targeting in 2000.

China's quest for economic intelligence (summed up perfectly in the Chinese philosophy of *Ping-zhan jiehe,* which, when translated, is to "combine peace and war") should be of particular concern to U.S. businesses from an insider security threat perspective.

During the height of the Cold War no other nation could match the desire and ability of the Soviet Union's KGB to steal American corporate secrets, particularly technology secrets. That has since changed, however. In today's world, China has replaced and improved upon the KGB model of industrial espionage to the point that China now represents the single most capable threat to U.S. technology leadership and national security.

The examples outlined thus far, however, lose their larger meaning and significance if not viewed from the overall perspective of China's orchestrated, government-backed industrial espionage program. When viewed through this lens, incidents that may appear to be isolated crimes based on an individual's desire for financial gain take on new meaning. The implications for corporate security and intellectual property protection are profound.

What we know thus far about China's espionage activities against U.S. weapons laboratories and other technology development programs is cause enough for concern. The U.S. intelligence community's official damage assessment of Chinese espionage targeting America's nuclear technology secrets tells us this much:

> — China obtained by espionage classified U.S. nuclear weapons information that probably accelerated its program to develop future nuclear weapons. This collection program allowed China to focus successfully on critical paths and avoid less promising approaches to nuclear weapon designs.
> — China obtained at least basic design information on several modern U.S. nuclear reentry vehicles, including the Trident II (W88).
> — China also obtained information on a variety of U.S. weapon design concepts and weaponization features, including those of the neutron bomb.
> — We cannot determine the full extent of weapon information obtained. For example, we do not know whether any weapon design documentation or blueprints were acquired.
> — We believe it is more likely that the Chinese used U.S. design information to inform their own program than to replicate U.S. weapon designs.

But there is much more to China's quest for U.S. technology. The People's Republic of China (PRC) has obtained a major advantage that the former KGB did not enjoy during the Cold War: unprecedented access to American universities and industry. At any given time there are more than 100,000 Chinese nationals in the U.S. attending universities and working throughout U.S. industry. Although many of these individuals are not spies, the fact remains that they are a major component of the PRC's industrial intelligence collection operation. In fact, some might be surprised to learn that there are very few professional PRC intelligence operatives actively working on collecting U.S. technology secrets compared to the number of PRC civilians who are actively recruited (either by appealing to their sense of patriotism or through other more coercive means) to routinely gather technology secrets and deliver those secrets to the PRC. Thus, the PRC employs a wide range of people and organizations to do its dirty work abroad, including scientists, students, business executives and even phony front companies or acquired subsidiaries of U.S. companies. During 1996, for example, more than 80,000 PRC nationals visited the U.S. as part of 23 different delegations and many likely were given specific collection requirements by the Chinese Ministry of State Security (MSS).

It is in the PRC where the military-industrial complex truly comes to life. Nowhere is this more evident than in the 1997 "16-Character Policy," which makes it official PRC policy to deliberately intertwine state-run and commercial organizations for the benefit of PRC military modernization. In their literal translation, the 16 characters mean as follows:

> **Jun-min jiehe (Combine the military and civil)**
>
> **Ping-zhan jiehe (Combine peace and war)**
>
> **Jun-pin youxian (Give priority to military products)**
>
> **Yi min yan jun (Let the civil support the military)**

The 16-Character Policy is important because of what it does for the PRC's industrial and economic espionage program: it provides commercial cover for trained spies who work directly for the PRC's military establishment. And their only mission in life is to gain access to and steal the high-tech tools and systems developed by the U.S. and its Western allies.

The two primary PRC organizations involved in actively collecting U.S. technological secrets are the Ministry of State Security (MSS) and the Military Intelligence Department (MID) of the People's Liberation Army (PLA). The MSS relies upon professionals, such as research scientists and others employed outside of intelligence circles, to collect information of intelligence value. In fact, some research organizations and other non-intelligence arms of the PRC government direct their own autonomous collection programs. Many of these so-called "princelings" — named for their political family connections within the PRC's Communist Party — use their political and business connections abroad to surreptitiously acquire technologies developed by U.S. firms. They employ a wide range of tactics, including managing covert collection operations, acquiring the assets of various U.S.-based commercial businesses, and even establishing front companies to gain access to sensitive and proprietary technologies.

Recent studies suggest that there are currently more than 3,000 corporations operating in the U.S. that have ties to the PRC and its technology collection program. Many are U.S.-based subsidiaries of Chinese-owned companies. And while in the past they were relatively easy to identify, recent studies indicate that many have changed their names in an effort to distance themselves from their PRC owners.

One case in 1993 involved a man named Bin Wu, who was convicted of transferring restricted night vision technologies developed in the U.S. to his MSS masters in the PRC. Wu, a pro-Western professor who once taught in China, had been given the option by the MSS of either helping them acquire sensitive technologies or going to jail for supporting the pro-Western Tiananmen Square uprising. He chose freedom and was instructed to travel to the U.S. and establish himself as a legitimate businessman.

Wu founded several front companies in the Norfolk, Virginia, area. He then actively solicited information from various U.S. companies and made many outright purchases of advanced technologies, including night vision equipment. The technologies were then shipped to the PRC.

U.S. investigations into Chinese espionage show that Wu was part of a much larger community of PRC sleeper cells. Many were not professional spies. Rather, they were simply business professionals or academics who were managed by MSS agents and given collection requirements based largely on the U.S. military critical technology list. In fact, during the 1990s these sleeper cells were used to establish front companies that would eventually target the Aegis missile system. In particular, the PRC seems to have been interested in acquiring the proprietary software that formed the basis of the command and control system for the Aegis.

In testimony before the Joint Economic Committee of the U.S. Congress on May 20, 1998, Nicholas Eftimiades, a former member of the U.S. intelligence community and the author of "Chinese Intelligence Operations," confirmed the organizational methods of China's industrial espionage program outlined above. According to Eftimiades:

> To collect technology and trade related information, China's premier intelligence services...co-opt vast numbers of Chinese citizens living or traveling overseas...
>
> First, co-optees are recruited in China and asked to acquire the targeted technologies while they travel abroad. Second, American companies with access to the desired level of technology are purchased outright by Chinese state-run firms. In intelligence circles this is considered a bold or aggressive operation. Third and most commonly, high-technology equipment is purchased by recruited agents running front companies. China's most productive method of legally acquiring foreign technology is to send scientists overseas on scholarly exchange programs.

> Much of China's espionage efforts in industrialized nations are focused on mid-level technology, that may or may not be cleared for export. The focus of this economic espionage on midlevel technology is because China's technological industrial infrastructure is still 10-15 years behind the United States...[32]

Many PRC domestic intelligence activities are directed against foreign businessman or technical experts. The data elicited from unsuspecting persons or collected by technical surveillance means is used by Chinese state-run or private enterprises. Prominent Beijing hotels, such as the Palace Hotel, the Great Wall Hotel, and the Xiang Shan Hotel, are known to monitor the activities of their clientele. In addition, the Ministry of Public Security (MPS) owns the Kunlun Hotel and probably monitors its guests. And anecdotal evidence provided to officials by Chinese prostitutes who frequent the Jianguo Hotel suggests that the guest rooms used by foreign businessmen contain microphones for eavesdropping. The Palace Hotel is owned in part by the PLA's General Staff Department. One of the American contractors for the Xiang Shan Hotel had a series of verbal battles with PRC officials as it was being built. The Chinese demanded that additional wires be installed in each room. The purpose of the wires was to tie in microphones.

.. -. ... .. -.. . / .--- --- -...

The new intelligence game is primarily about economic competitiveness. And it is a trend that is not likely to change anytime soon, according to the Office of the National Counterintelligence Executive report. In fact, even during times when new innovations in the IT industry were scarce, the demand for information technology trade secrets continued unabated. And the reason for that is clear: investment in information technologies has a direct correlation to a company's potential market capitalization. IT is the new gold standard.

Former CIA director Robert M. Gates told a conference of business executives in Oct. 2000 that the so-called "business spy threat" is real and growing. "They want technological production and marketing information, and they usually share what they get with their country's companies. To get this sensitive information, government intelligence services use many of the techniques developed during the Cold War," he said.[33] These techniques include bugging telephones and breaking into the hotel rooms of U.S. businessmen and businesswomen, and even planting moles in companies to steal or surreptitiously download files. And as you will see later in this book during our discussion of the security surrounding the Department of Energy and America's nuclear weapons secrets, Chinese nationals (who may be working at the behest of their government) continue to pose a significant threat.

The case of Junsheng Wang and Bell Imaging offers an interesting example of the melding of international espionage and the threat to proprietary trade secrets. On April 26, 2001, Wang and Bell Imaging pled guilty to theft and copying of trade secrets belonging to Acuson Corp. A related company, Belson Imaging Technology Company Limited, a joint venture based in the People's Republic of China, was also charged in the case with copying trade secrets. In pleading guilty, Wang and Bell Imaging admitted that Wang took without authorization and copied for Bell Imaging a document providing the architecture for Acuson's Sequoia ultrasound machine. According to Wang's plea agreement, he had been able to obtain access to the Acuson trade secret materials because his wife was employed as an engineer at the company and she had brought the document into their home. Wang said he copied the document and took it with him in 2000 on business trips to the People's Republic of China for Bell Imaging. Wang was arrested carrying documents containing Acuson trade secrets at San Francisco International Airport as he was about to board a flight for Shanghai.[34]

In September 2004, the FBI arrested 34-year-old Yan Ming Shan, of Daqing, China, on charges that he deliberately accessed, with the intent to defraud, computers and proprietary software belonging to 3DGeo Development, Inc., a Mountain View, Calif.-based company that develops software used to survey land for sources of natural gas and oil. Shan was arrested as he was about to board a flight to China.

3DGeo employed Shan from April through Sept. 2002 under an agreement with one of its customers, PetroChina, a Chinese company with a division named DaQing Oil. Shan routinely traveled to California for training on 3DGeo's software. However, on Sept. 11, 2002, two 3DGeo employees noticed Shan creating a large electronic master file consisting of multiple files that the company considered proprietary trade secrets. Shan then changed the attributes of the file so that it became invisible. The two 3DGeo employees then searched through the files that Shan had placed in the master archive and discovered that the files contained proprietary software source code and programs that Shan was not authorized to have access to. And although all of the files were protected by passwords, company officials discovered that Shan had used a software cracking program to uncover the passwords, which he then stored in a master file on his personal laptop computer.

According to the criminal complaint against Shan, the information he obtained represented "the root value of 3DGeo and is not a product that 3DGeo would ever sell or disclose without very specific use restrictions."[35] On December 16, 2004, U.S. District Court Judge Jeremy Fogel sentenced Shan to prison for two years minus time served while awaiting trial.

Chinese government-owned companies have also been involved in schemes to steal the intellectual property of U.S. companies. And they have done this using the corporate equivalent of sleeper cells — foreign executives hired by U.S. companies on work visas, as well as naturalized American citizens who then establish U.S. companies for the purpose of gaining access to the proprietary data of other U.S. firms.

The U.S. Department of Justice on May 3, 2001, arrested and charged two Chinese nationals and a naturalized Chinese-American citizen with conspiring with a Chinese state-owned company to steal proprietary source code and software from Lucent Technologies Inc. As of this writing there has been no court decision in the case. However, according to the federal indictment, Hai Lin and Kai Xu, both of whom were employed at Lucent as "Distinguished Members" of the company's technical staff, colluded with Yong-Qing Cheng, a naturalized American citizen and vice president of a U.S. optical networking company, to form a new business based in Beijing, China, using stolen Lucent technology.

The criminal complaint filed against the three executives alleges that they approached a Chinese state-owned company, named Datang Telecom Technology Co., seeking to establish a joint venture, which they stated in an e-mail would become the "Cisco of China." Lin, Xu and Cheng then formed a company called ComTriad Technologies Inc., and with $1.2 million in funding from Datang, the two companies formed DTNET — a joint venture approved by Datang's board of directors. There was just one problem. The Internet-based voice and data services product that Lin, Xu and Cheng were developing on behalf of the new venture (dubbed the CLX 1000) was based entirely on the proprietary software in Lucent's PathStar Server, a product that earned Lucent more than $100 million during the previous year. It also was the very same technology that Lin and Xu had been working on while employed by Lucent.

Justice Department prosecutors allege that FBI searches of the computers used by the defendants reveal that on Jan. 21, 2001, Lin sent an e-mail to a representative of Datang advising that the "bare src" – allegedly referring to a portion of the PathStar source code – had been transferred to the ComTriad password-protected Web site, and that more source code would follow.

While it is not clear if Lin and Xu became aware of an investigation into their dealings or if they simply became paranoid, once the Lucent source code had been uploaded to the Web the two defendants began taking steps to hide their association with ComTriad. According to the Justice Department, they removed their names from the publicly-filed ComTriad articles of incorporation and obtained a post office box as the new mailing address for ComTriad. In addition, Cheng removed his name from an Internet registry record linked to the password-protected ComTriad Web site (www.comtriad.com) and Lin and Xu began using ComTriad e-mail addresses that did not identify them by name. They also used their wives' names to obtain cell phones for ComTriad business. Lin and Xu then went as far as to assume the aliases Howard Lin and Roy Xu when communicating with the public regarding ComTriad business.

All three men were arrested on May 3, 2001 at their homes in New Jersey. When FBI agents searched their houses they seized large quantities of the component parts of the PathStar Access Server, including software and hardware, as well as schematic drawings and other technical documents related to the PathStar Access Server marked "proprietary" and "confidential." Among other things, the agents seized a modified PathStar machine from Lin's basement. Although presumed innocent until proven guilty, all have been indicted by a grand jury in Newark, New Jersey.

In a superseding indictment announced by prosecutors on April 11, 2002, the damage caused by this alleged economic espionage case goes well beyond Lucent. According to prosecutors, several other companies had licensed portions of their proprietary technology to Lucent for use in the PathStar Access Server. Those companies included Telenetworks, a business unit of Next Level Communications, headquartered in Rohnert Park, Ca.; NetPlane Systems, Inc. (formerly Harris & Jeffries, Inc.), a wholly-owned subsidiary of Mindspeed Technologies, Inc., headquartered in Dedham, Mass.; Hughes Software Systems, Ltd., a division of Hughes Network Systems, Inc., headquartered in Gurgaon, India; and ZiaTech Corporation, a wholly-owned subsidiary of Intel Corporation, headquartered in San Luis Obispo, Ca.

"This was a grave intrusion upon American business and technology," said U.S. Attorney Robert J. Cleary in a statement shortly after the arrests were made. "In the information age, it is difficult to imagine anything more dangerous to a company's business interests."[36]

As is evident from the above case, individual acts of economic espionage can impact multiple companies. That was certainly the case in November 2001, when FBI agents arrested two San Jose, Calif.-based businessmen as they were about to board a plane to China carrying suitcases full of trade secret documents totaling more than 8,800 pages and $10,000 in equipment that they had allegedly stole from four U.S. high-tech companies.

When FBI agents arrested Fei Ye and Ming Zhong, they discovered microchip blueprints and computer aided design scripts from Sun Microsystems Inc., NEC Electronics Corp., Transmeta Corp. and Trident Microsystems Inc. Both once worked at Transmeta and Trident. Likewise, Fei Ye also worked at Sun and NEC. Prosecutors alleged that both men, originally from China, planned to use the stolen technologies to start a microprocessor company with the assistance of the Chinese government.

According to the indictment filed on December 4, 2002 in a U.S. District Court in the Northern District of California, Ye and Zhong established Supervision Inc. (a.k.a Hangzhou Zhongtian Microsystems Company Ltd., and a.k.a Zhongtian Microsystems Corp.) to sell microprocessors in China. They also allegedly sought the direct assistance of the Chinese government and stated in their corporate charter that their company would assist China in its ability to develop super-integrated circuit design, and form a powerful capability to compete with worldwide leaders in the field of integrated circuit design.[37]

Although the indictment does not charge any government entity of China, it does suggest that there was considerable interest in and potential support from the Chinese government. A so-called "panel of experts," for example, found that the Supervision project had "important significance" for China's high-level embedded CPU development program and integrated circuit industry, and recommended that "every government department implement and provide energetic support."[38]

.. -. ... .. -.. . / .--- --- -...

Why put all of this effort into spying on private companies? The answer to that question is simple.

Researchers estimate that during the late 1990s, companies of all sizes and across industries in the U.S. collectively invested more than $1 trillion in so-called "intangible assets" — research and development, software development, business process reengineering, patents, branding, customer databases, trade secrets, human know-how, and other forms of intellectual capital that do not appear on a firm's financial balance sheet. And, if we once again apply the Big Bang theory of information technology we get an ever-expanding universe of intellectual capital that resides primarily in electronic form.

Some studies, such as those conducted by the American Society for Industrial Security, PricewaterhouseCoopers, and the U.S. Chamber of Commerce, have suggested that more than 70% of the market value of a typical U.S. company is derived from intangible, digital assets and intellectual property. In fact, Investopedia.com, an investment education Web site, conducted an analysis of Intel Corp. and found that while the company's pre-tax earnings from 2001 to 2004 amounted to roughly $9.5 billion and its tangible assets were valued at approximately $37.6 billion, the value of the company's intellectual capital – value that does not appear on its balance sheet – was approximately $35.3 billion.[39] What this teaches us is that Intel Corp., and many other high-tech firms like it, is actually a research and development company whose intellectual capital enables it to produce microprocessors.

According to Baruch Lev, a professor of accounting and finance, of every six dollars of market value, only one dollar appears on a corporate balance sheet, while the remaining five dollars represent intangible assets.[40] And investment in IT systems has a substantial impact on market valuation due to IT's ability to transform organizations and feed intellectual capital generation.

"While a dollar of physical investment (property, plant, equipment) is valued in the capital market at approximately one dollar on average…computer capital is associated with close to ten dollars of market value," according to Lev. "Explanation of the high valuation associated with computers is that they reflect the value (contribution) of organizational capital, not just of computers."[41]

It should be no surprise, therefore, that intellectual property (invariably stored in the form of electronic data) has become the central target of foreign intelligence agents working on behalf of their nation's industry, as well as unscrupulous employees, contractors and criminals seeking to turn their access to such data into financial gain.

.. -. ... .. -.. . / .--- --- -...

In 1999, the American Society for Industrial Security (ASIS) surveyed 45 Fortune 500 companies and found that on average America's corporate economy lost more than $45 billion a year as a result of theft of trade secrets and loss of proprietary data. The average loss reported by the Fortune 500 enterprises surveyed that year was estimated to be more than $500,000 per incident. More telling, however, was the conclusion that trusted employees or contractors accounted for more than 75% of all thefts of intellectual property.

In a similar study sponsored by the FBI and conducted by the Pacific Northwest National Laboratory, an economic loss model estimated that intellectual property thefts and misappropriation of proprietary data resulted in more than $600 million in lost sales and the loss of approximately 2,600 full-time jobs per year.

Yet another study conducted at the time by the Computer Security Institute found that nearly 20% of the 585 companies surveyed said that they were victims of trade secret information theft. And 66 of those companies reported financial losses of more than $66 million – the most costly crime noted in the survey.

By 2001, ASIS revised its survey findings, placing the cost of proprietary information loss at more than $59 billion.[42] Likewise, the largest average dollar loss per incident ($404,000) involved theft of research and development (R&D) data. Furthermore, the most commonly reported areas of risk reported by the companies were R&D (49%), customer lists and data (36%) and financial data (27%).[43] These same companies said the greatest risk factors directly contributing to intellectual property losses were former employees, foreign and domestic competitors, and on-site contractors.

.. -. ... .. -.. . / .--- --- -...

As a postscript to our discussion of the new espionage, a live risk assessment conducted last year by Reconnex Corp. at a major federal agency revealed that nation states are not the only potential problem when it comes to insider espionage and sabotage. Terrorism is yet another threat.

During the risk assessment at the major federal agency (the name of which is being withheld for security reasons) counterintelligence officials discovered e-mail communications from a trusted employee to an unidentified individual located in the financial district of Manhattan. The content of the e-mails revealed a potential plot to "use the [federal agency's] network to support al-Qaeda."

The incident remains hidden behind a thick wall of secrecy. However, the author was present during a briefing that described for the agency's counterintelligence staff the technical aspects of how this particular insider was uncovered. And while it would be inappropriate to discuss the specific details of this person's identity, job function and location within the federal government, officials told the author that "personnel actions" had been initiated.

News Story

E-mail glitch exposes private data in California

The incident could be the first major test of the state's privacy law

News Story by Dan Verton

JULY 06, 2004 (COMPUTERWORLD) - IT officials in Contra Costa County, Calif., today launched a countywide investigation into how hundreds of internal e-mails containing private employee data were sent out inadvertently to a Swedish company.

The investigation was launched after *Computerworld* notified the county that Robert Carlesten, a 26-year-old managing director of Internet company Ord & Bild, based in Karlstad, Sweden, could produce dozens of e-mails he said have been arriving at his Internet.ac domain regularly for the past two years.

Carlesten said he had tried to contact the senders of the e-mails on numerous occasions but received no reply.

In addition to a deluge of administrative communications from the county's Department of Information Technology and human resources director, the e-mails contain detailed discussions and attachments related to the payroll files for the county's Superior Court as well as current and former employee benefits. Many of the e-mails, obtained by *Computerworld*, contained the names, employee numbers and benefits of Superior Court commissioners and other workers.

Tom Whittington, CIO of Contra Costa County, said the county became aware of the problem only after receiving calls from *Computerworld*. A preliminary investigation, he said, revealed that the problem was the result of some county employees using erroneous e-mail address books and wasn't caused by a virus or worm infection.

"We've started to take action to stop this, and I believe we have stopped it," said Whittington. "We shut off and blocked the Internet.ac domain so our employees can't send any e-mails to that address."

Part of the problem, said Whittington, is that the county's naming structure includes ".ac" for the auditor controller's office. "Now we need to research who has the bad address book that has this address."

But that move poses a potential challenge for Whittington's IT administrators: Many employees have personal address books that are stored only on their PCs, making it impossible for the county's IT department to centrally update all address books.

Although Whittington said he has been advised by the county's chief information security officer that counties and cities are exempt from California's landmark identity-theft law, known as SB 1386, some legal analysts said the county may be required to notify those whose personal information was compromised.

SB 1386, which went into effect July 1, 2003, requires companies that do business with California residents to inform customers when their names, in combination with personally identifiable information, have been accessed by an unauthorized person. If Contra Costa County is required to follow the statute, it would be the first major test of the law.

Jeff Matsuura, a professor at the University of Dayton School of Law, said that on face value, the e-mails appear to contain personally identifiable information that is covered by SB 1386. "It seems to me that such an incident would gut the statute if this kind of disclosure did not fall within it," said Matsuura.

He added that there might be other federal legal issues that come into play, such as whether the incidents violate the Electronic Communications Privacy Act.

"If I were advising the county, I'd tell them to notify everybody whose personal data was compromised," said Matsuura.

Chapter 3

The Malicious

"Almost all of these people are loyal at the time of hiring, so this isn't a matter of screening them out."
– Jerrold M. Post, former CIA Psychologist

T he case of Timothy Allen Lloyd offers a good example of how psychological stressors and triggers can play a role in malicious insider attacks.[44] It is also the very first insider sabotage case investigated by the U.S. Secret Service.

For 11 years, Lloyd worked his way up the corporate ladder at Omega Engineering Corp., a Bridgeport, New Jersey—based manufacturer of high-tech industrial process measurement and control devices for the U.S. Navy and NASA. He started with the company as a machinist, but by 1994 he had earned the title of chief system administrator for the company's Novell network.

But Lloyd's career was about to take a drastic turn for the worst. Employees reported that he repeatedly elbowed, shoved, and bumped colleagues in the hallways, and that he became verbally abusive. He would be counseled on several occasions about these problems, but managers reported that he never improved his behavior. In May 1995, because of his continuing interpersonal problems, Lloyd's supervisor, James Ferguson, informed him that he was being transferred from supervisor of Omega's CNC Department (the manufacturing side of Omega's plant, where machines created the thousands of products that comprised Omega's inventory) to a position as a manufacturing engineering support specialist. Ferguson assured Lloyd that this was a lateral move. In reality, the change was a demotion. And Lloyd knew it. The loss of supervisory responsibilities and the knowledge that Courtney Walsh, a former subordinate of Lloyd's, had taken over his position did not sit well with Lloyd.

Lloyd's supervisors had hoped that the change of position would send Lloyd the message that his behavior and social skills had to improve. They also hoped that the job change would help spur that improvement. But it had the opposite effect on Lloyd, and his interpersonal problems with fellow workers increased in number and severity.

Lloyd underwent a performance appraisal in Feb. 1996. He received a ranking of 7 out of a possible score of 10. He received a 4% cost of living raise in salary, which was significantly lower than the annual raises he received in previous years. The intent of Lloyd's managers was to send the signal to the troubled employee that his time left at Omega was short.

Four months after his performance appraisal, Lloyd instituted a policy to "clean up" all of the computers in Omega's CNC Division. The "policy" forced all employees to save their work on a centralized file server and prohibited them from making their own backups. Lloyd also removed portions of computer programs that deal with safety precautions from user workstations and saved them on a central file server. Walsh protested, fearing that removing the files from user systems could cause a major system failure. Lloyd, however, continued making the changes.

By July 1996, Lloyd's behavior had become too much of a liability for Omega's management. As a result, Ferguson and another Omega manager met with Lloyd on July 10 and informed him that his history of interpersonal problems with managers and fellow employees, including incidents of intimidation, could no longer be tolerated. He was fired on the spot and escorted out of the building.

Shortly after 8 o'clock in the morning on July 31, technicians at Omega informed Ferguson that the division's file server would not boot up. They tried everything they could think of. Nothing worked. Finally, Ferguson made the decision to reload the system from the emergency backup tapes that were maintained under lock and key in the human resources department. So to the human resources department he went. But when he got there he couldn't believe his eyes. The secure file cabinet was empty. The emergency backup tapes, which stored the company's 1,000 manufacturing and tooling programs, were gone.

Ferguson called Lloyd on the telephone. He was frantic.

"Tim, Tim, do you have the backup tapes?" Ferguson asked frantically.

Lloyd said he didn't have the tapes and that he had left them in his desk drawer at Omega.

"Tim, we need those tapes. Are you sure you don't have them?"

"No," said Lloyd.

Ferguson then hired local data recovery experts to help retrieve the critical files that had been deleted. To their dismay, the files had been purged and rendered unusable. The purge had been accomplished by somebody with supervisory level access to the system and was clearly intentional as far as the experts who were assisting Omega were concerned. And at Omega, there was only one Novell system administrator with supervisory level access. And that one person was Timothy Lloyd.

On August 23, the U.S. Secret Service executed a search warrant of Lloyd's home and recovered two Omega emergency backup tapes that had been reformatted, a master hard drive from another Omega system and various other pieces of hardware and software belonging to the company — nearly 700 pieces of evidence in all.

Eventually, data recovery experts from Ontrack Data International began the painstaking process of digging through the electronic ground zero that was now Omega's file server. They were searching for evidence to support the Secret Service's strong suspicion that Lloyd had deliberately obliterated the company's files. The clue that told them this was a deliberate act came from six strings of data that, when taken together, pointed to Lloyd and to a deliberate act of sabotage.

First, the technicians uncovered a date — the day before the catastrophe struck. The next item was a supervisory logon account (12345 with no password). They then discovered a line of code that referred to all of the data stored on the server and a "/Y" command that instructs a program to default to "yes" when confronted with a logic expression. Finally, the last thing that the Ontrack experts discovered was the "purge" command followed by "F:\," which pointed to the Omega server and everything on it.

Then things got really interesting for the Ontrack investigators. They uncovered a mysterious command named FIX.exe, which was not a known Novell executable file. Upon testing the DOS-based command DELTREE.exe, which allows an administrator to delete files from a Microsoft Windows operating system, they discovered that DELTREE.exe returned the expression "Fixing..." rather than "Deleting..." Somebody had modified the DELTREE.exe file to disguise its true function. The user, therefore, would have no clue as to what was actually happening to the system.

This was literally the 'ticking time bomb' that the Secret Service was looking for. It was a logic bomb designed to go off upon boot up regardless of which user logged onto the system. And to the delight of the Secret Service, the same time bomb code that had obliterated Omega's file server was found on one of Lloyd's personal hard drives that had been confiscated during the search of his home. The Secret Service had their man.

The government prosecutor told the jury that it could not have been anyone other than Lloyd who could have conducted such an organized, well-planned and rehearsed attack on the Omega file server. "Was the real guy sitting next to Tim Lloyd and fiddling with the system and changing dates?" the prosecutor asked the jury. "I suggest not. Who could do all this and not be questioned by the administrator? No one. It was the administrator. He was setting this up months in advance. This was his parting shot to a company he was leaving, a going-away gift. . . . And it was almost a perfect crime."

Lloyd's lawyer challenged the prosecution's witnesses on almost all accounts and even produced ten former Omega employees who testified that they had never witnessed or were made aware of behavior problems relating to Lloyd. In addition, Lloyd gave Network World magazine an exclusive interview in which he denied having anything to do with the incident and also denied having ever been a system administrator.

The jury deliberated for 12 hours over the course of three days. They convicted Lloyd on one count of computer sabotage and acquitted him on the other count related to transportation of stolen goods.

On Feb. 26, 2002, a judge sentenced Lloyd to 41 months in prison, three years of probation and ordered him to pay more than $2 million in damages to Omega. But that was a paltry sum compared to the actual damages incurred by the company. Executives testified that Lloyd's actions cost the firm $10 million in damages and another $2 million in re-programming costs. In addition, 80 Omega employees lost their jobs as a result of the financial damages caused by the attack.

It is clear that Lloyd had determined months in advance that his job was in jeopardy. He also seems to have made a conscious decision at that time to begin shaping the battlefield for his ultimate, decisive offensive — the logic bomb. Once again, the victim organization had ample evidence preceding the attack that should have indicated Lloyd was an at risk employee for malicious insider behavior. The company's lack of action on that front suggests, as does the lack of action by other organizations studied thus far, that the existence of policies and procedures rarely serves as a deterrent to a dedicated and motivated insider adversary. Likewise, although written policies that delineate potential repercussions for unethical or unauthorized computer activity may act as a moderate deterrent for the average, honest end-user, such policies and penalties have proven impotent in the face of a committed insider, especially one who has experienced a "trigger" event that moves him from contemplation to action.

The implications of this for those contemplating how to develop an effective insider defense are quite significant. What this tells us is that from an insider threat perspective the age-old security equation of 'Security = People + Process + Policy + Technology' may need to be adjusted, placing a heavier weighting on technology. The insider threat is the one area of security where people, process and policy have rarely, if ever, proven to be an effective deterrent.

Based on the Lloyd case we also see evidence that management (people, process and policy) failed to interpret Lloyd's previous behavioral problems as a potential security risk to the company's IT and electronic assets. Despite repeated warnings, both written and verbal, Lloyd's managers continued to trust him, and him alone, with full, exclusive administrative access and duties. Some have suggested that Lloyd's managers at the time were preoccupied with the company's global expansion and, therefore, had relegated security concerns to the bottom of their priority list. This certainly seems to have been the case. However, this may have also been a factor in Lloyd's decision to shift his feelings of disgruntlement into action.

The process of shaping the battlefield includes conducting probing attacks. These are low-level skirmishes intended to help the attacker determine enemy strengths and weaknesses, and can be a key component of intelligence collection. The concept of the probing attack pre-dates the electronic world by centuries; however, the electronic world of hackers has adopted this time-tested method to its advantage. And it is clear that Omega had ample evidence that Lloyd had been conducting these types of attacks. And his success, coupled with the lack of any real management intervention, reinforced his sense of invincibility.

.. -. ... .. -.. . / .--- --- -...

Our study of the modern, high-tech insider shows us that the computer age has had an impact on ethical norms in the workplace. But how much of an impact is still unclear. Some studies suggest that an individual's normative beliefs and the ethical climate throughout his place of employment have the most influence when it comes to determining ethical or unethical behavior. Other studies have also found that one's sense of moral obligation combined with awareness of consequences for not acting in an ethical manner were key to the process by which IT students determined an act to be ethical or unethical.

There may also be differences between how men and women act when confronted with questions of ethical or unethical behavior in an IT setting. For example, a study of IT students (average age 22 years) enrolled at a major Midwestern university revealed that males were more likely (57%) to use an employer's computer resources on the weekend to develop applications for friends than were women (42%).[45] In addition, women showed a greater intent to act ethically across the spectrum of all ethical scenarios.

According to the authors of the above study, "the individual's degree of favorable evaluation of the behavior, their moral judgment and individual reasoning, the obligation to do something about the act, the individual's strength of conviction, their gender, and the situation (scenario) are factors that explain the intention to behave ethically/unethically."[46]

Some experts have taken this research and argued that because there are so many intangible human factors involved in determining who will and will not act in an ethical manner when using IT systems that the obvious solution is to institute comprehensive programs focusing on policy enforcement and awareness of the repercussions that could stem from different levels of unethical behavior. For example, some argue that employees should be made aware that low-level misuse of IT resources can and likely will be punishable through docking of pay or official written reprimand. But we've already seen cases where malicious insiders faced certain prison sentences (in the case of international espionage, life sentences) and still acted unethically. It is because of this fact — that policies and threats of punishment often do not deter the dedicated malicious insider or the insider who has little fear of being caught — that technical controls must be employed. And those technical solutions must not only search for anomalies in usage patterns, but they must also focus on the data that the organization considers most sensitive.

What the Pollard, Ames, Hanssen and Lloyd cases teach us is that a system of formal controls based upon policy and procedure is worth little more than the paper it is printed on without a technical enforcement mechanism. Therefore, a data-centric, technology-based solution should be considered the core element (the first and last line of defense) of an internal security strategy. It is your insurance policy for the inevitable: people (management and employees), policy and process will fail.

"One-hundred percent of our risk assessments have shown a failure or breakdown of internal controls, including people, policies and processes," said Reconnex's chief e-Risk assessment leader Daniel Smith.

News Story

Theft charges filed against four former Microsoft workers

The government alleges they stole $32M worth of software

News Story by Todd R. Weiss

NOVEMBER 15, 2004 (COMPUTERWORLD) - Four former Microsoft Corp. employees have been charged with theft, conspiracy, mail fraud and money laundering in connection with the alleged theft and resale of $32 million of Microsoft software.

In a case filed by the U.S. attorney's office in Seattle on Nov. 8, the four former Microsoft employees allegedly took advantage of an internal company program that provided any Microsoft software products free to employees as long as the goods were for business use. Instead, the four workers, Finn W. Contini, Robert A. Howdeshell, Alyson M. Clark and Christine J. Hendrickson, all of whom live in the Seattle area, allegedly requested thousands of software products through the internal program and then sold them for personal gain, according to the 33-page criminal complaint filed against them.

Contini and Howdeshell have unpublished telephone numbers and couldn't be reached for comment. Clark and Hendrickson also couldn't be reached for comment.

Contini, Clark and Hendrickson worked as group assistants at Microsoft, while Howdeshell was a project coordinator, according to the complaint. All four workers had access to the free internal software program, the government alleges.

Contini worked for Microsoft from September 1999 to February 2002, and Howdeshell worked there from May 2000 to October 2001. Clark worked for the company from June 1992 until last month, and Hendrickson worked there from March 2000 until June 2002.
The government alleges that Contini ordered 5,400 software products worth $17 million through the employee program, while Howdeshell ordered 985 products worth $4 million. Clark allegedly ordered 618 products worth $1.7 million, and Hendrickson ordered 1,726 products worth $9.7 million. Overall, the value of the alleged thefts was about $32.4 million, according to the complaint.

The software included copies of Microsoft Windows XP Professional, Windows Advanced Server 2000, Exchange Server Enterprise 2000, SQL Server 2000 and SharePoint Portal Server 2001. The government alleges that the four former employees earned more than $3 million from the sale of the products to middlemen, who then sold them on the secondary market.

Chapter 4

The Disgruntled

"Any intelligent fool can make things bigger, more complex, and more violent. It takes a touch of genius – and a lot of courage – to move in the opposite direction."
– Albert Einstein

F oreign intelligence agents operating on U.S. soil and within U.S. institutions are by no means the only malicious insiders Americans should be concerned about. As we've seen in the examples of Pollard, Ames and Hanssen, America produces a steady flow of home-grown insiders who are willing to abuse their public trust. And as we will see with their private sector counterparts, these insiders have proven once again that security in the electronic age requires much more than strict policies and ironclad procedures. Security also requires proactive monitoring and enforcement mechanisms; for the disgruntled are forever plotting their revenge.

Thomas A. Varlotta is a case in point. Between 1993 and 1998, Varlotta headed a team of four software developers responsible for designing the code that powered a critical automated system used to relay flight information between the air traffic controllers at O'Hare International Airport and controllers at the Elgin, IL, Terminal Radar Approach Control (TRACON) facility. The project cost the Federal Aviation Administration $1 million.

During the six years that he worked on the project, Varlotta gradually moved up the pay scale, eventually earning the equivalent of a GS-14 government civil servant. But in May 1998, officials informed Varlotta that his pay grade was about to revert to a GS-13 equivalent. Within a month, Varlotta decided he would resign from his position and take the only existing copy of the software with him. A confidential source told federal prosecutors that after learning of his pay change Varlotta said he planned not to finish the project as a means to force the FAA to pay him what he thought he deserved.

Federal officers recovered the software code during a raid on Varlotta's home in Tinley Park that August, but it was encrypted with a 13-digit password. Experts at the National Aeronautics and Space Administration said it would take as long as 400 years to unscramble.

Varlotta pled guilty to a single felony count of code theft in September 2000. "He intended to hold the FAA and O'Hare Airport hostage," prosecutors argued.

On June 12, 2001, U.S. District Judge William Hibbler sentenced Varlotta to a one year prison term.

"Three years ago I made the biggest mistake of my life," said Varlotta. "I have lost my job, my career and the respect of my peers."[47]

Varlotta's expression of genuine remorse was a rarity among disgruntled insiders.

.. -. ... .. -.. / .--- --- -...

On Feb. 26, 2003, a grand jury in Pennsylvania indicted Kenneth Patterson on two counts of password trafficking and computer damage. Patterson was a former employee of American Eagle Outfitters, the popular designer, manufacturer and seller of a brand of clothes for 15- to 25-year-olds. The company has 774 stores in the U.S. and 70 stores in Canada. At the time of the indictment against Patterson, the company had reported a sales record for the month, bringing in more than $74 million.

In late Oct. 2002, American Eagle Outfitters in Marshall Township, Pennsylvania, fired Patterson from his position as a data communications manager. The firing stemmed from his role in an incident with an e-mail server that has not been made public. The former IT worker then planned to get his revenge. And he timed his operation to coincide with the most hectic time of the year for retailers across the nation.

The day after Thanksgiving in the United States is known as "Black Friday." It is the official beginning of the Christmas holiday shopping season and, more importantly, the day that most retailers count on to get out of the red and into the black. For American Eagle Outfitters, however, "Black Friday" 2002 would take on new meaning.

For two days starting on Nov. 27, the company fought for its electronic life. Somebody had launched a denial of service attack on American Eagle's computer network. The attack prevented the retail giant from processing credit cards during the busiest time of the holiday shopping season. The perpetrator turned out to be Kenneth Patterson.

In addition to conducting the attack, Patterson went to a public library and used its Internet access to post the user names and passwords of legitimate American Eagle employees on a hacker bulletin board. Prosecutors described Patterson's actions as malicious and calculated, and added that the denial of service attack cost the company at least $70,000.

In his defense, Patterson argued that he was under the influence of alcohol at the time of the incident and that his judgment had been severely impaired. And while that is certainly possible, he acknowledged in court feeling regret and remorse at what he had done.

U.S. District Judge Gustave Diamond sentenced Patterson to 18 months in prison and ordered him to pay American Eagle Outfitters $64,835 in damages.[48]

News Story

Source code stolen from U.S. software company in India

Jolly Technologies blamed an insider for the theft

News Story by John Ribeiro

AUGUST 05, 2004 (IDG NEWS SERVICE) - Jolly Technologies, a division of U.S. company Jolly Inc., reported yesterday that an insider at its research and development center in Mumbai stole portions of the source code and confidential design documents relating to one of its key products. As a result, the company has halted all development at the center.

Jolly Technologies is a vendor of labeling and card software for the printing industry. It set up its R&D facility in Mumbai less than three months ago, according to a statement from the parent company.

The company said that according to a report obtained from its branch in India, a recently hired software engineer used her Yahoo e-mail account, which now allows 100MB of free storage space, to upload and ship the copied files out of the research facility. The company detected the theft and is trying to prevent the employee from further distributing the source code and other confidential information.

The vast majority of U.S.-based software companies require their employees to sign an employment agreement that prohibits them from carrying the company's source code out of a development facility or transferring it in any way.

Though the Indian branch of Jolly Technologies requires employees to sign a similar employment agreement, the sluggish Indian legal system and the absence of intellectual property laws make it nearly impossible to enforce such agreements, the company said.

Representatives of San Carlos, Calif.-based Jolly Technologies in Mumbai are working closely with local law enforcement authorities, seeking their assistance in taking corrective action against the employee and to prevent such crimes from occurring again.

The company said it has decided to delay further recruitment and halt development activities in India until better legal safeguards are in place.

Chapter 5

The Outsourcing Powder Keg

"Once a company tells employees their job will be outsourced, they don't usually keep them around because there is the risk of the employee seeking revenge and damaging company property or projects."[49]
– Anonymous Source

The concept of loyalty is changing in America. One might go as far as to argue that loyalty in the American workplace has been at a crossroads for several years. The outsourcing of American technology jobs has left many skilled citizens searching for work, struggling to feed and clothe their families, and losing sleep over an uncertain future while watching lower-wage workers overseas prosper. And while U.S. companies temporarily halted their plans to outsource jobs in the immediate aftermath of the Sept. 11, 2001 terrorist attacks, the trend is now once again in full swing. This has led to an undercurrent of anger and resentment throughout the American IT workforce.

The trend of outsourcing IT jobs overseas has added new pressures to the highly volatile mix of ingredients that go into the making of a disgruntled or malicious insider. This is a topic that has until now gone unnoticed. But the American company ignores this potential powder keg at its own peril.

How much IT development work has moved from Main Street U.S.A. to Europe and the Far East? The answer, if you consider recent statistics, is quite a lot. In Oct. 2004, for example, International Data Corp., a consultancy in Framingham, Mass., estimated that U.S. companies outsourced $6.87 billion worth of custom application development, systems integration and application management. More than 72% of that work went to India, 8% went to the Philippines, 7.7% went to Central and Eastern Europe, and China took in 6.5%. Consulting firm Gartner Inc. estimated that by the end of 2004 one out of every ten U.S. IT jobs had been shipped overseas.[50]

Other studies are more telling. The TPI Index, for example, put the value of IT outsourcing contracts signed during the first quarter of 2005 at $10.8

billion.[51] In addition, Forrester Research Inc. predicted at the time of this writing that by 2015 3.5 million white-collar jobs, or 200,000 per year, would move out of the U.S. to offshore locations. In fact, some estimate that between 2000 and 2003 approximately 104,000 IT jobs were lost in the U.S. to offshore outsourcing.

And contrary to popular belief, U.S. companies aren't shipping only low-level jobs overseas. While there are plenty of low-level call center jobs that are now based in places like India, there is also an alarming new trend taking shape where research and development work is increasingly being sent overseas. For example, 70% of the personal digital assistants (PDAs) and 65% of the laptop computers on the market today are designed in Taiwan. And even networking infrastructure leaders, such as Cisco Systems, Nortel and Lucent, are increasingly farming out critical software design work to overseas firms. Wipro Technologies, for example, employs 8,000 researchers and developers to produce telecommunications equipment, electronic systems for automobiles and microchips for various industries. It is the world's largest contract R&D firm. And it is based in India.[52]

Cellon International, one of the world's largest independent wireless design firms, is also one of the few such companies based in the U.S. However, the San Jose, Calif.-based firm has major testing and development facilities in China and France.

Still not convinced that R&D work has left the United States? Then consider the marked drop in R&D budgets at some of America's leading technology firms. Hewlett-Packard Co., that famed American high-tech firm founded in a garage, now spends a measly 4.4% of its budget on in-house (or, "in-garage") R&D. Dell's R&D budget is well below 1% and has been dropping steadily since 2001.[53] It is the undeniable reality of the present economy: American corporations have outsourced America's innovative spirit, and in doing so have sent the message to America's high-tech workers that they are no longer valued or necessary. This is not a political statement. It is the current perception of a large swath of the American workforce. And perceptions are reality.

More important, however, the companies that are responsible for this outsourcing have acknowledged being highly concerned about employee backlash stemming from the loss of U.S. jobs. In fact, 84% of those companies surveyed by IDC said they had such concerns.

And that backlash may come from both those who have been outsourced and those who survive the ordeal. In fact, outsourcing survivors may react with outrage, fear, or survivor's guilt. Others may respond to the ordeal with a heightened work ethic, bordering on manic behavior, say psychologists and workplace consultants. Those workers whose jobs are not lost can also sometimes develop what experts consider low-level post-traumatic stress disorder. This type of reaction, which can be the "trigger" that leads to lashing out against the organization, is often the result of loss of influence in the work-place, loss of control over one's own destiny and a feeling that the organization does not respect or value one's presence.

On the low end of the threat spectrum, outsourcing has sometimes led to loss of worker productivity and management difficulties. For example, some managers have alluded to working under a "black cloud" after an outsourcing deal had been struck. From there, however, problems can escalate to stock price fluctuations and even malicious actions by once-trustworthy insiders.

The outsourcing of America is a raw wound that has been left untreated and is now infected with resentment. Nowhere is that more evident than in the annals of the Communications Workers of America union, which is leading a massive public relations campaign to inform American workers where their jobs have gone. A look at the language and characterizations used to describe the practices of outsourcing and hiring of foreign visa workers reveals a level of anger that is on the verge of exploding.

The practice of outsourcing to overseas locations and hiring foreign H-1B visa workers has been called "The American Worker Replacement Program" by members of the CWA. The new American corporation has been likened to the slave owner of the early 19th Century, and the foreign worker as an inden-tured servant. Even the likes of Enron have come under fire for its use of foreign workers. More important, however, the average American company has been demonized because of the increase in overseas outsourcing and hir-ing of foreign workers, and is now characterized as an Enron waiting to happen. Consider the following posted on the CWA Local 4250 Web site and written by Glenn R. Jackson, chairman of the American Reformation Project and a senior manager in the IT industry:

> While Enron has been castigated for the destruction wrought by its corrupt business practices on its employees' 401K's and [the] job losses, the truth is that this terrible final chapter was already in the cards years earlier. Enron, like many of America's Corpora-tions, had during the late 1990's been developing a distain [sic] for the American worker, and instead finding an addiction to foreign workers through the H-1B visa program.
>
> The American worker is in trouble. American corporations rec-ognize only loyalty to the corporate shareholder and increasing share valuations, missing the point that shareholders and investors are one and the same with their corporate employees. The truth of course can almost always be found by following the money, and the immigration story is no different. Lowering salary expenses to im-prove the corporate bottom line and receive the reward from Wall Street is the name of the game. Remembering Main Street and the workers that make it all work is no longer a priority.[54]

American industry and the American workforce, particularly the Ameri-can IT workforce, are in the middle of a nasty divorce in which both parents are threatening to abscond with the only child — the American job. But what impact is this battle having on the concept of loyalty? And is the perceived negative impact something that companies and government organizations need to worry about from an insider security perspective? These are difficult questions to answer, but the overall perception of the problem of unemployment in high-tech America is that it has become a battle between good and evil. In fact, the modern American corporate enterprise (and to a certain extent federal, state and local government institutions that have also outsourced jobs) increasingly is seen as an immoral entity bent on denying social justice for the American worker in favor of higher shareholder value. Perhaps more than ever, today's American worker feels like little more than a cog in a machine that no longer reads "Made in America."

Reinforcing this notion is the fact that outsourcing has increased in the face of both rising unemployment and a growing foreign trade deficit. In fact, the U.S. economy lost more than 1.5 million jobs between 1989 and 2003 due to increased trade with China — a country that actively targets U.S. industrial and national defense secrets. At the end of 2004, the U.S. unemployment rate stood at 5.4%, or 8.15 million workers. In addition, Forrester Research forecasts that 3.3 million white-collar jobs, mostly technical positions, and approximately $136 billion in earnings will move overseas by 2015.

Consider the following anecdotal evidence collected by the online site The Royal Forum.

> An anonymous source explained the social stress placed on her father after learning his job was going to be outsourced before retirement. "I have seen him get depressed, watched his health decline and searched for a smile when he references his work over the past year and a half. When a person dreads going to work and fears walking away from a retirement built over 20+ years, there is a lose-lose situation for the company's image and the employee's well-being and right to a healthy work environment." These conditions [are often magnified] in loyal and good employees with feelings of remorse and distrust of the company. A source told The Royal Forum, "Once a company tells employees their job will be outsourced, they don't usually keep them around because there is the risk of the employee seeking revenge and damaging company property or projects."[55]

In a letter to the editor of CIO Magazine, a reader reveals the level of anger about outsourcing that currently infects the minds of many American workers. "About that pore [sic] CIO who has the recurring nightmare. He should be more then [sic] worried about Americans boycotting his company's products," wrote the reader. "He should fear for his life. Bullets after all are cheap here in the good old USA."[56]

A CIO Magazine article that appeared on Sept. 1, 2003, described a meeting of T.O.R.A.W. (The Organization for the Rights of American Workers), during which angry unemployed IT workers vented their frustrations. John Bauman opens the meeting by saying the issue is "about our jobs, our homes, our families." Then the rhetoric gets heated. One attendee at the meeting calls H-1B visas "a tool of the devil" and goes on to berate the "corporate greed of CEOs that is ruining this country."

A reader who responded to the article mentioned above, agreed with the characterizations offered by the members of T.O.R.A.W. "Any CEO, CIO, or CFO that tells us they are doing a service to us by sending this work offshore, whether in IT or in manufacturing are traitors to this country and frankly, are a greater long term danger than the likes of Osama Bin Laden," he wrote. "Foreigners bleeding money from this country are their cohorts, and until we replace those people in our government who have aided and abetted in this treason, we will inevitably see the complete demise of the great American economy."[57]

It should also be acknowledged that some workers view the fight against globalization and outsourcing as a patriotic duty and those companies that engage in outsourcing as disloyal. Some say offshore outsourcing is destroying America.[58] Likewise, some IT workers have said they will boycott U.S. technology producers in favor of foreign producers like Sony. Why? In the words of one IT worker, "at least [Sony and other foreign companies] are employing their countrymen."[59]

Don Tennant, the editor-in-chief of Computerworld, shared with the author some of the angry letters that many IT professionals have written to him in response to an editorial he wrote on the issue of outsourcing. On November 15, 2004, Tennant wrote an editorial titled "Get Over It," in which he describes those who oppose offshore outsourcing on patriotic grounds as "xenophobes" and reactionaries.

> I received a thought-provoking e-mail in response to my column two weeks ago in which I thanked IT professionals for their perseverance, and I just had to share it:
>
> "Sir: It is interesting that on page 18 of the 11/01/04 *Computerworld* you 'thank' the community of IT professionals, yet on page 37 of the same issue you print another 'how-to' article advising corporate traitors on how best to destroy the jobs of those same professionals. Your hypocrisy is disgusting."
>
> That article, as you might have guessed, dealt with outsourcing. But it was only tangentially about offshoring, so I hate to think how disgusted this reader would have been if we had devoted the entire story to the taboo topic. He probably would have lost his lunch.

It's an amazing dynamic we have here. That was only one of count-less e-mails we've received in recent years suggesting that sending work offshore is anti-American. And more often than not, we're charged with being equally anti-American for writing about it. (Our outsourcing special report, which begins on page 39, will no doubt fan that flame.) There's an intense, reactionary disdain for these "corporate traitors" among a very vocal element of xenophobes, and IT professionals -- vendors and users alike -- are increasingly reluc-tant to incur their wrath.

Last May, I interviewed Mark Barrenechea, executive vice presi-dent of product development at Computer Associates, and asked him about the development work that CA has elected to do off-shore. The strategy Barrenechea described seemed reasonable and prudent to me, but I could tell he was uncomfortable talking about it. When I said I wanted to move on to a new topic, Barrenechea, visibly relieved, laughed. "I would welcome it!" he bellowed.

That dynamic was apparent a couple of weeks ago during a panel discussion I moderated at a gathering of IT services providers. One panelist, Denny Brown, vice president and CIO at Arizona Public Service Co., said he limits offshore outsourcing to no more than 10% of his development work. The reason: "To pass the newspaper test," Brown said, only half joking. What he meant was that having word get out via the media that you're offshoring more than 10% is to be avoided.

And who can blame him? Nobody has the time or inclination to deal with torrents of venomous e-mail. But I have three words for anybody who takes the outlandish position that sending work off-shore makes you a turncoat: Get over it.

Rather than griping, try doing something innovative that's going to keep you and your colleagues employed. That's what Brown did. A former executive at IBM Global Services, Brown has adopted that group's model by transforming his IT shop into a services provider that competes against outside vendors to do work for his company's business units. That customer-oriented approach has worked well enough to give him the economic means to pass the newspaper test. Another panelist, Tom Ault, a senior vice president at electronic components distributor Avnet, said his company's business is cycli-cal, following the ups and downs of the semiconductor market. So during the down times, Avnet becomes an outsourcer itself by mak-ing its underused IT resources available to other companies. IT departments that are innovative enough to generate revenue tend to keep jobs from going elsewhere.

The point is that companies may outsource a lot of things, but innovation isn't one of them. Making excuses for a failure to recognize that is what's *really* disgusting.

Tennant's rant did not go unheard. His readers responded in kind. Although the names are being withheld in respect to the writers' wishes for privacy, the following examples come directly from the mainstream IT profession and represent an undercurrent of virulent resentment toward the modern American corporation and the government that allows it to send U.S. jobs overseas.

Letter 1:

I can't believe that any American would write such trash. How can you support sending up to 250,000 Americans to the unemployment [sic] line annually because corporations can get the work done for third-world prices elsewhere? I am certainly not threatened by losing my job to outsourcing, but I am an American and I don't like the direction that outsourcing is taking our country or economy. Anyone who cannot clearly see the evidence of how this is adversely affecting our country is blinded by their own greed.

If you love India so much, move there. You won't be missed. Oh, you can't because they are overpopulated and you won't be able to find work? Tough! They should have exercised a little control in their breeding habits instead of popping out offspring like rabbits generation after generation.

Letter 2:

I'm bummed that Don Tennant doesn't understand the nature of the H-1B visa. If it truly were about hiring qualified workers, rather than flooding the market with cheap labor, [the regulation] would not be written to give the sponsoring employer the power of a feudal lord. And how about balancing this flood of labor with job opportunities for Americans in other countries?

I'm bummed that Mr. Tennant chooses to present the concerns of American workers as xenophobia. Who's going to pursue a career in Science or Engineering if they can be replaced by a serf?

And finally, I'm bummed that Mr. Tenant chooses to ignore widespread unemployment in tech. I WISH this were a simple competition of qualifications and experience, but jobs are leaving this country in pursuit of lower salaries, not better skills.

Letter 3:

Don overlooks that H-1B [workers] are not always the "most qualified." Employers often force the "most qualified" Americans to train the H-1Bs before firing them.

Don overlooks that the majority of positions filled by H-1B [workers] could easily be filled by U.S. workers.

Don overlooks that flooding in 85,000 workers per year into a stagnant job market WILL cause qualified U.S. workers to be displaced. The H-1B destroys supply and demand. Supply and demand must operate   within   a closed system. Don offers no explanation why the free market within the U.S. cannot supply enough U.S. tech workers without immigration.

Don overlooks that many highly skilled workers have been sending hundreds of resumes without a single offer, and finally leave the profession in desparation [sic].

Don overlooks that the CEO of HP lobbied for an increase of the H-1B cap even as she was filing and [sic] SEC notice of layoffs.

Letter 4:
Your article entitled "The Three Stooges" strongly implies that [the People's Republic of China] is a benign, friendly, peace-loving nation with only the best intentions. That is such BS, that I had to gargle with Listerine after reading your tripe. Let's see, Red China up to its eyeballs in the food-for-oil scandal run by the UN. And, let's not forget, the human rights violations that are well documented by Amnesty International. Oh, oh, and let's remember that they have dozens of ICBM's targeted at the US mainland with guidance systems - supplied a la the Clintonistas - fully capable of vaporizing most west coast cities and many other US cities.

Yes, to be sure, Red China is our greatest friend and only the myopic could think anything differently. It's assholes like you that make me hate this industry that I have dedicated to a thirty-year career. Go peddle your horseshit/bullshit elsewhere; we're all loaded up here!

Letter 5:
Before I begin, I would like to tell you a bit about myself. I have been working in high tech for the past 11+ years. While in some people's eyes, this may be considered to be "junior" in many regards, I am writing this in response to your letter to your readers on November 15, 2005.

The concept of outsourcing can be made into a complex quagmire where you can place blame on everyone but yourself or you can take it the simple way where you can blame it on executives and the political climate. Regrettably it is sad to see that the all mighty dollar [sic] (which is incidentally becoming weaker by the second) is somehow clouding your view as well as your readership.

It is commendable that you can have a writer who says that he doesn't blame big business for offshoring and he can go anywhere he wants, but unfortunately if you take it to its logical extreme, not only is that not true, but it's a dangerous belief to think that. We are not in a true free market economy as evidenced by companies who hire professional lobbyists and token Americans to show that they are actually the "good guys" who can brainwash mediocre CEOs like Carly Fiorina, Bill Gates and Larry Ellison into thinking that cutting costs for inferior work is actually a GOOD thing.

In this day and age of trying to foster competition for better, faster and cheaper we are shortchanging ourselves when we can look at CXOs and have them laugh at the fact they offshore and it's acceptable. Perhaps they forgot the day that they tried to get a job or remember every day that their jobs are in the balance, perhaps they think that there is always another job - but when you offshore your labor, you lose your edge – you lose your Intellectual Property and many times the rewards you get are infinitely less than when you started in house.

As someone who is currently working in a startup, I find it disheartening that Corporate America has to cheat itself in order to compete in this war against competition. The US cannot afford to sit and laugh while its technology seeps away to the lowest bidder with no accountability. CEOs who do this should be willing to take a pay cut and be paid like their lowest paid employee like many other countries and not lauded like Gods and Goddesses for selling their souls and getting huge bonuses for doing bad things not good for their company and the economy as a whole.

Keep in mind I am not saying that internationalization is bad – I strongly believe we need to increase our mindshare in markets like China, India and the like, but as long as they don't play fair (and you know exactly what I mean by that), is it really fair for us to look at them to rape us blind (and I do mean rape - we are being tied down and being treated very poorly for what?) and then ask for more.

I am a free marketeer first and an American, but it doesn't mean that they are mutually exclusive. This country is taking a serious gamble by doing this and you should be at the forefront telling companies to get the government, universities and other places to promote free market economics, not government regulated oligopolies!

This is not a question of good or evil as you put it or a simple case of corporate treason, this is a case of our future that is truly at stake here and the US probably does not want to become a third world nation - so why promote this zero sum game?

Think long and hard at what I am saying here... and I look forward to hearing a reply from you. If I don't, I will just assume that you either don't know or don't care about the ramifications of your magazine - because they are much deeper than you think.

Letter 6:
I read with interest your editorial on 7 February entitled "The Three Stooges". Lord knows I've no confidence in this congress making any   sort of informed decision on technical issues.

But your article seems to be trying to convey the impression that there's absolutely nothing to worry about, and I don't think that's realistic, either. My concern isn't with national security, but rather loss of technical hardware and especially software intellectual property. U.S. companies seem to think they can deal with the Chinese government and Chinese corporations (effectively, the same thing) on the same basis they deal with other U.S. companies--that contracts are binding, and that agreements protecting intellectual property, trade secrets, etc. will be honored.

Experience is being painfully gained--too slowly--to disabuse them of that belief. There is no perceived disadvantage to violating such agreements as soon as it is of benefit to either China itself or the Chinese corporate entity involved, and nothing will be done by the current administration to invoke [World Trade Organization] WTO or other sanctions to protest such violations.

I wouldn't let any process, procedure or sensitive information that I valued ever be transferred to a Chinese corporation; I can only hope that the executive management of U.S. companies will learn to carefully examine and consider any agreements that release such information to "partners" in China.

Letter 7:
Bad enough outsourcing has severely weakened the industrial might that won wars for us. Now you put personal gain over patriotism, you deserve a traitor fate. I would love to watch that.

Letter 8:
I meant to blast you for your earlier piece of trash, which bad-mouthed unemployed American IT workers (like myself) as whiners and complainers, but I held my tongue. But since you've

once again proven what a complete jerk you are, I no longer feel compelled to restrain myself. Once again, you've written an article that is totally uninformed, and 180 degrees out of phase with what most Americans believe. If your aim was to provoke outrage, you've succeeded at that. The only true statements you made were that China spies on us, and is one of our largest trading partners. However, you conveniently left out the following facts:

1) China is a communist country, which has no regard for intellectual property rights owned by American companies.

2) China steals billions of dollars a year from American companies by producing counterfeit goods, which their government refuses to crack down on, because it benefits them.

3) China is one of the world's worst human-rights violators, and doesn't allow its citizens any basic rights or freedoms (remember Tiananmen Square?).

4) China's communist legacy, under Mao [Tse-tung], is one of mass murder - an estimated 20 million Chinese opposed to communism were executed during Mao's reign, yet Mao is still considered a national hero in China, and there are still many statues honoring him.

5) China constantly threatens to invade and destroy democratic Taiwan, a United States ally we are pledged by treaty to defend.

6) China's military, especially their navy, sees the United States as their main enemy, and wants to kick us out of Asia completely.

7) China keeps its currency artificially low, pegged to the U.S. dollar, which helps them, and hurts the United States economy. They also refuse to remove their dollar peg, despite pleading from the United States and the [European Union] EU.

8) China holds a disproportionate amount of US treasury bonds to "help us" finance our huge trade deficit with them, which gives them too much control over the United States economy.

9) China has a very low-paid labor force that U.S. corporations are exploiting, by shipping American factories and jobs to China. Once again, this helps China, and hurts the United States economy and workers.

10) Chinese spies at Los Alamos, like Wen Ho Lee, have stolen all of United States' atomic weapons research, including our latest atomic weapon designs. (Author's Note: Wen Ho Lee was officially acquitted of espionage.)

11) China owns the Panama Canal through their holding company Hutchison Whampoa, which gives them strategic control over a key U.S. Navy choke point.

12) China has signed oil and gas energy agreements with Iran and communist-run Venezuela - moves aimed at undercutting the strategic interests of the United States.

13) China and Russia recently signed a military pact, with the aim of defeating the United States in a future military conflict.

I could go on and on, but the above points are just a few of the facts you conveniently left out of your article. You are either a complete fool, with absolutely no knowledge of geopolitics and military issues, or you simply choose to ignore the facts. Since I don't think it's possible that a former NSA employee can be *that* dumb, I suspect that you are deliberately malicious, and have an agenda.

Your article "The Three Stooges" once again clearly illustrates that you *do* have an agenda – one that is not in the best interests of our country. You are obviously one of the "free trade at all costs" people, who don't give a damn what harm it causes to the United States. You are just another silver-haired corporate lackey, toeing the corporate line. Why, I wonder? Could it be because IDG, Computerworld's parent company, is heavily involved in outsourcing, and makes a lot of money from it? FYI, that is a huge conflict of interest for Computerworld, and it makes *you* the real stooge, not any member of Congress – they are pointing out a genuine threat from China; one that is growing rapidly, thanks to companies like IBM and Microsoft, and corporate stooges like you. Companies like IBM and Microsoft, and corporate stooges like yourself who front for them, are little more than traitors, because you are helping to build up a hostile communist dictatorship which views us as their main enemy. News flash to corporate stooge: we may be at war with China in the near future, and your traitorous articles don't help the situation at all.

It makes me wonder what excuses you will come up with when the United States economy and way of life have been completely destroyed, thanks to muddle-headed, short-sighted trade policies espoused by corporate stooges like yourself. I suppose you will blame *that* disaster on American workers and the U.S. government, as well. You would obviously never blame our "wonderful" communist Chinese trade partners, who poke *us* in the eye at every opportunity, not the other way around, as you claim. Maybe you should move back to China and stay there, because you seem to have more loyalty to communist China than to your home country. It's little wonder that you no longer work for the NSA – you were probably selling their secrets to the Chinese. Maybe that's why they subjected you to so many polygraph tests. You also previously mentioned that your son is in the Navy. Being in the Navy, he should have a more realistic view of the genuine military threat represented by China. Maybe you should consult with him, before writing your next piece of knuckle-headed, traitorous trash.

P.S. Do not print my letter in Computerworld. I don't want my name and letter to be on your web site for all eternity, in case we are living under a Chinese/Russian occupation force in the future. That may yet happen, thanks to people like you. Shame on you!

P.P.S. I've taken the liberty of copying your CEO on this letter. He needs to know about the traitorous crap that you've been spewing out, under the Computerworld banner. It is truly disgraceful.

Letter 9:
It is interesting that on page 18 of the 11/01/04 Computerworld you "thank" the community of IT professionals, yet on page 37 of the same issue you print another "how-to" article advising corporate traitors on how best to destroy the jobs of those same professionals. Your hypocrisy is disgusting.

Letter 10:
I have been offered early retirement (their term, I call it being laid off) by my company. When that happens, and it's happening a lot, I'll have to cancel my subscription. Enough cancellations and YOU will be 'retired' too. No one GETS OVER life shattering events.

Letter #8 struck a chord with the author given my former professional relationship with International Data Group (IDG) and its chairman, Patrick McGovern. As an eight-year veteran of IDG and a former senior writer for Computerworld magazine, the flagship publication of IDG, the author often found it difficult to come to terms with IDG's deep involvement in China and that country's horrid track record on human rights. The IDG chairman was among the first U.S. business leaders to do business in China and remains, to this day, among the most influential U.S. businessmen in China. In fact, McGovern and IDG are so influential in the Chinese market that IDG initially published Cosmopolitan Magazine in China on behalf of Cosmo. Today, however, there are more than 50 U.S. magazines with Chinese language editions. But McGovern has stated in the past that China would likely become the biggest market for IDG, which already publishes 28 titles there.

On May 9, 2005, Computerworld's Tennant interviewed Gerald Cohen, the founder and CEO of New York-based business intelligence software vendor Information Builders Inc. Tennant asked Cohen about his position on outsourcing and H-1B visa workers. And in his usual outspoken fashion, Cohen held nothing back.

"Bill Gates told an audience in Washington recently that the U.S. needs to get rid of the cap on H-1B visas. What's your position on that?" asked Tennant.

"He's full of it," said Cohen. "He says, 'I'd hire a lot more American engineers if I could find them -- they're not available, and that's why we're going to China and India'. He's going there because it's just cheaper. He can find all the engineers he wants in this country."

But "a lot of CEOs at companies like yours are saying that they just can't find the people," responded Tennant.

"That's bull," said Cohen, whose firm outsources quality assurance work overseas. "You know who wants [to get rid of the cap on H-1B workers]? The Indian companies. The way the Indian companies work is they have to have a certain number of people here, and a lot more people back there - so they're the ones who want to get all these people in. And they don't even pay them American wages -- they just pay them as cheaply as they can."

But where does offshore outsourcing and the H-1B visa debate come into play in our study of the insider threat? That's simple. Many of the cases studied by Post and Shaw, for example, involved trusted insiders who lashed out at their employer shortly after learning that they had been selected for termination, demotion or reassignment. Post and Shaw correctly characterize these types of personnel actions as "catalysts" for malicious behavior by those who are part of the at-risk group. For example, in one case a project manager was demoted and reacted in anger to the demotion by e-mailing project plans to a competitor.

Many psychologists and workplace counselors acknowledge that job terminations (including demotions or reassignments that stem from outsourcing) set off a grieving process that begins with anger and resentment. And often there are psychological precursors to malicious insider activity that go unnoticed by senior managers leading up to a major attack on the last day of employment.

Therefore, insider attacks responding to the loss of a job or demotion that stemmed from outsourcing decisions can be placed in what Post and Shaw call the *Machiavellian* and *Avenger* categories. While these categories were crafted to describe different types of insider characteristics, both can be applied to the general threat stemming from employee backlash to outsourcing decisions.

Machiavellians, according to Post and Shaw, use their employer's systems and networks "ruthlessly to advance their personal and career goals." Examples include those who used logic bombs to establish consulting careers or to use as insurance against being fired; some framed their bosses to advance or protect their careers. Some may steal intellectual property to jumpstart what they perceive is the inevitability of having to succeed at a new position.

Avengers, on the other hand, often react directly to a personal or professional setback, such as losing work to an offshore source of cheap labor. These individuals are overcome with an extreme sense of bitterness, which can lead to a range of actions including sabotage, theft, extortion and even espionage. In one example offered by Post and Shaw, a system administrator who had heard she was about to lose her job at a major healthcare provider as a result of a downsizing effort encrypted the organization's patient files. She then offered to fix the problem in return for a severance package and a non-prosecution agreement signed by the healthcare provider. Faced with few alternatives, the healthcare provider agreed to the employee's terms. And in doing so, the company forfeited all legal ability to press charges afterward.

.. -. ... .. -.. / .--- --- -...

The outsourcing phenomenon has also re-defined the concept of the insider. Today's insiders not only live on Main Street, U.S.A., but in places like Mumbai, India. Because that's where an ever increasing number of U.S. technology companies are outsourcing their research, development, testing and quality control work.

American technology companies have outsourced such work to Indian firms for years. And the trend is in a constant upswing. As we've already seen, the cost of labor in places like India is just too enticing for many American technology developers to ignore. Even if the security of their intellectual property and, at times, the crown jewels of their companies are at stake.

The problem facing most companies that outsource their development and design work overseas is that there is little or no verification of the backgrounds of the workers who are being granted access to source code and other proprietary technologies. While many American executives at some of the nation's largest and best known technology firms have tried to put a positive spin on their foreign outsourcing initiatives, the cold, brutal reality is that they have done little to verify what individuals are working at these overseas facilities, and even less to verify and control their access and conduct.

In May 2003, I raised the issue of offshore technology development to a panel of senior IT executives during a security conference in Myrtle Beach, S.C. The research firm Gartner Inc. had just released a study that predicted within a year more than 80% of U.S. firms would begin to consider outsourcing critical IT services, including software development, to foreign companies in places like India, Pakistan, Russia and China. But to my surprise, I was not alone in my sense of astonishment at the naiveté demonstrated by America's captains of industry. The vast majority of the attendees at the conference – average technology users – also expressed dire concern at the U.S. technology industry's complete disregard for the facts surrounding the targeting of American intellectual property and technologies.

Of particular concern to many of the attendees was the IT development work that was being sent to China. Audience members also expressed significant concern about plans to send work to countries in Southeast Asia, particularly Malaysia and Indonesia, where terrorist networks are known to exist.

Speaking directly to Oracle Corp. Chief Security Officer Mary Ann Davidson, one audience member said it was "ironic that the countries the software industry trusts the least with binary code are the places where source-code development is being sent."

Putting her best game face on, Davidson acknowledged to the crowd that Oracle, which sells its software to all of the major U.S. intelligence agencies, sends some of its development work to companies in India and China. However, "we give read access, not write privileges, to developers in India," she said. "And for the work done in China, it's quality control, and they do not need source-code access to do that."

Davidson, however, acknowledged that there is "a national security issue" involved in moving development work overseas. But the economic situation today is such that "you can't build these products without non-U.S. citizens," she added. "Whether you like it or not, our national secrets are already being preserved by people who built these parts of the core infrastructure, and they're not U.S. citizens."

During the closing session of the conference, an informal survey was taken. Attendees were asked if they believed U.S. companies would follow through on what was clearly a pressing requirement to conduct security assessments at their overseas outsourcing facilities. The results were clear: the majority of attendees doubted the ability or willingness of U.S. software companies to conduct proper background investigations of foreign software coders working overseas.

That was not surprising, said Joyce Brocaglia, CEO of Alta Associates Inc., an executive search firm. "I'm surprised at how few of my clients actually do background checks on their information security professionals," she said. "At most, they require me to do a reference check."

It was not one of American industry's finest moments.

The informal survey conducted at that conference revealed more than America's lack of faith in the wisdom of its technology and business executives; it showed that these executives truly are incapable of acting against a threat unless it is staring them in the face.

In April 2005, however, the incident that everybody had been warning high-tech America about finally happened. Police in Pune, India, arrested three former employees of a call center on charges they defrauded four Citibank account holders in New York out of $300,000. The three alleged perpetrators worked for Mphasis BPO, the business process outsourcing operation of Bangalore-based software company Mphasis BFL Group. Police in

India charged them with collecting and misusing account information from customers they dealt with as part of their work at the call center.

Less than a week after news of the Mphasis Three broke, Indian technology firms announced a plan to begin an employee screening program. As of this writing, the National Association of Software and Service Companies in Delhi plans to launch a pilot program of an employee registry in June 2005.

One of the major problems that the project will have to overcome, however, is the lack of a centralized database in India that collects information on credit records and other personal history data. It was only last year, for example, that the first credit bureau in India, the Credit Information Bureau of India Ltd., was formed.

Despite these problems, India is the next home of the American IT industry, said Cohen. "If you look further down the road, there's going to be a huge drain of IT jobs," he told Tennant during their interview. "A lot of these jobs that go overseas are the spawning grounds for future jobs. So the whole industry's going to move offshore. I guarantee you [that] if it doesn't stop in a couple years you're not going to have much of an IT industry here."

News Story

Seagate: Ex-employee can't work for a rival

It wants a court injunction to stop him from working for Western Digital

News Story by Robert McMillan

AUGUST 09, 2004 (IDG NEWS SERVICE) - Hard drive maker Seagate Technology LLC is seeking a court injunction to prevent a former employee, Pete Goglia, from going to work for Western Digital Corp., saying Goglia knows too much about Seagate's hard drive reading and writing technology to work for a competitor.

"This particular employee, who has been here for a very long time, has extensive knowledge of proprietary and confidential information," said Brian Ziel, a Seagate spokesman. "We believe he will inevitably disclose some of that proprietary information that he has gained through working at Seagate."

Goglia worked at Seagate for 17 years. Most recently, he was executive director of its recording-head operation. He left the company July 30 and is scheduled to start work at Western Digital today, Ziel said.

Seagate filed an injunction Friday with Minnesota State Court for Hennepin County, seeking to keep Goglia from working on Western Digital's read/write technology for two years, Ziel said. "We're not saying he can't work there in that division forever," he said.

In July 2003, Lake Forest, Calif.-based Western Digital acquired the assets of storage head maker Read-Rite Corp. for $95 million. Scotts Valley, Calif.-based Seagate is concerned that Western Digital will continue to develop the Read-Rite technology using trade secrets owned by Seagate, Ziel said.

Western Digital declined to comment for this story.

Chapter 6

The Government Insider

"In short, the trusted insider betrayed his trust without detection."
— FBI Director, Louis Freeh, Feb. 20, 1991

Ramon Garcia was born in Chicago on April 18, 1944. He was a quiet young man, introverted and an intellectual of sorts. As an undergraduate at Knox College, he studied chemistry and Russian. Then he went on to study dentistry at Northwestern. By 1971, he had completed the requirements for a Master's degree in Accounting and Management Information Systems. Two years later, he earned his certification as a public accountant.

But a year employed as a junior accountant at a public firm in Chicago had its downside. For one thing, it was boring work – even if pushing paper and crunching numbers behind a desk suited one's quirky and reclusive personality. So in 1972, Ramon decided to make a change. He joined the Chicago Police Department and became an investigator in the Financial Section of the Inspection Services Department. It wasn't the special weapons and tactics (SWAT) unit, but it was better than being a run-of-the-mill downtown accountant.

After four years with the Chicago PD, Ramon once again got the itch to reach for the next level. On January 12, 1976, he entered duty as a Special Agent with the Federal Bureau of Investigation, holding a Top Secret security clearance. After his initial training, Ramon was detailed to the FBI's Indianapolis Field Office, where his accounting and information systems background led him to the White Collar Crime Squad. The future was looking bright for the young Ramon. The FBI had seized upon his unique educational background and was making good use of it. Ramon was doing the type of work he was cut out for, even if he wasn't the easiest guy to get along with or the most talkative guy in the office. There seemed to be no limit to how far a smart guy like Ramon could go in the bureau.

By the summer of 1979, Ramon had been detailed to the New York City Field Office. He initially worked in accounting – his area of expertise – but by the following March he began working on intelligence matters. Because of his experience with computers, Ramon's first official assignment was to help establish the N.Y. Field Office's automated counterintelligence database. The new database represented a sea-change for the FBI. It was new technology, and was having a profound impact on the way counterintelligence investigations were managed. Its contents, which included biographical data on hundreds of foreign diplomats and intelligence agents living and working in the United States, were classified Secret. Ramon's work on the database was generally considered a success.

The early 1980s brought a new round of changes for Ramon. He was now working at FBI headquarters in Washington, D.C. For a brief time he worked intelligence matters as a Supervisory Special Agent, but soon returned to budgeting work, managing the FBI's piece of the National Foreign Intelligence Program. Once again, Ramon found himself preparing budget justifications. Only this time his work was being read and acted upon by the Congress of the United States.

Despite the mundane nature of his work at headquarters, Ramon's budgeting responsibilities gave him access to the entire gamut of data pertaining to FBI intelligence and counterintelligence operations. This would come in handy in 1985, after Ramon had been transferred to the Soviet Analytical Unit, the mission of which was to provide senior policy makers and other analysts throughout the intelligence community with analysis of Soviet intelligence operations inside the United States.

Ramon's career was back on track. His number-crunching days had once again given way to real FBI work involving access to Sensitive Compartment Information (SCI) – among the most highly classified programs in the U.S. intelligence community. Before being granted access, however, Ramon was forced to undergo SCI indoctrination training and sign a special access agreement. The agreement Ramon signed read in part:

> ...I have been advised that direct or indirect unauthorized disclosure, unauthorized retention, or negligent handling of the designated Sensitive Compartmented Information by me could cause irreparable injury to the United States and be used to advantage by a foreign nation...
> ...I have been advised that any unauthorized disclosure of the designated Sensitive Compartmented Information by me may be a substantial violation of this agreement, and may result in the termination of my employment.

At this time, Ramon also began serving as a member of the FBI's Foreign Counterintelligence Technical Committee, which was the body responsible for coordinating and managing technical surveillance and eavesdropping operations against foreign intelligence agents operating in the U.S. Everything Ramon touched turned to gold. His career was moving forward and appeared to be on a rapid upward progression. Ramon was not only living the American dream, he was among the brave few whose job it was to protect and defend it. And for a talented FBI agent looking for action there was no better place than the New York Field Office. And Ramon was heading back.

.. -. ... .. -.. / .--- --- -...

On October 4, 1985, a brief rain shower passed through Northern Virginia as Viktor Degtyar checked the mail at his Alexandria, Va., home. It seemed to be the usual array of junk mail. But one parcel stood out from the others. It was austere and unadorned with the usual return address. The only clue to its sender was the postmark: October 1, 1985, Prince George's County, Maryland.

Viktor opened the envelope, only to find another envelope. But on this envelope, there was a message:

DO NOT OPEN. TAKE THIS ENVELOPE UNOPENED TO VICTOR I. CHERKASHIN.

Degtyar knew immediately what could be at stake. Victor Cherkashin, after all, was the KGB[60] Line KR (Counterintelligence) officer at the Soviet embassy in Washington. Degtyar was his political (Line PR) counterpart.

Cherkashin opened the envelope, revealing an unsigned typed letter that read as follows:

DEAR MR. CHERKASHIN:
    SOON, I WILL SEND A BOX OF DOCUMENTS TO MR. DEGTYAR. THEY ARE FROM CERTAIN OF THE MOST SENSITIVE AND HIGHLY COMPARTMENTED PROJECTS OF THE U.S. INTELLIGENCE COMMUNITY. ALL ARE ORIGINALS TO AID IN VERIFYING THEIR AUTHENTICITY. PLEASE RECOGNIZE FOR OUR LONG TERM INTERESTS THAT THERE ARE A LIMITED NUMBER OF PERSONS WITH THIS ARRAY OF CLEARANCES. AS A COLLECTION, THEY POINT TO ME. I TRUST THAT AN OFFICER OF YOUR EXPERIENCE WILL HANDLE THEM APPROPRIATELY. I BELIEVE THEY ARE SUFFICIENT TO JUSTIFY A $100,000 PAYMENT TO ME.
    I MUST WARN OF CERTAIN RISKS TO MY SECURITY OF WHICH YOU MAY NOT BE AWARE. YOUR SERVICE HAS RECENTLY SUFFERED SOME SETBACKS. I WARN THAT MR. BORIS YUZHIN, MR. SERGEY MOTORIN,

AND MR. VALERIY MARTYNOV HAVE BEEN RECRUITED
BY OUR "SPECIAL SERVICES."[61]

The author of the letter then described in precise detail a Top Secret SCI-level program involving eavesdropping techniques being employed by the U.S. National Security Agency (NSA) against the KGB. In addition, to "further support my bona fides" the author outlined specific secrets about recent Soviet defectors to the United States. The letter continued:

DETAILS REGARDING PAYMENT AND FUTURE CONTACT
WILL BE SENT TO YOU PERSONALLY...MY IDENTITY
AND ACTUAL POSITION IN THE COMMUNITY MUST BE
LEFT UNSTATED TO ENSURE MY SECURITY. I AM OPEN
TO COMMO SUGGESTIONS BUT WANT NO SPECIALIZED
TRADECRAFT. I WILL ADD 6, (YOU WILL SUBTRACT 6)
FROM STATED MONTHS, DAYS AND TIMES IN BOTH
DIRECTIONS OF OUR FUTURE COMMUNICATIONS.

The package arrived on October 15, as promised. Degtyar opened it and found dozens of classified documents, some of them originals, from throughout the U.S. intelligence community. The next morning, at 8:35, an FBI surveillance team observed Degtyar arrive at the Soviet embassy carrying a large black canvas bag – an unusual item based on Degtyar's routine and the first major clue that the Soviet "diplomat" may have made contact with a traitor in the U.S. government.

The next letter arrived at Degtyar's Alexandria, Va. residence on October 24. It outlined directions for the KGB to deliver payment to its newly-found ally in the U.S. intelligence community.

DROP LOCATION

Please leave your package for me under the corner (nearest the street) of the wooden foot bridge located just west of the entrance to Nottoway Park. (ADC Northern Virginia Street Map #14, D3)

PACKAGE PREPARATION

Use a green or brown plastic trash bag and trash to cover a waterproofed package.

SIGNAL LOCATION

Signal site will be the pictorial "pedestrian crossing" signpost just west of the main Nottoway

Park entrance on Old Courthouse Road. (The sign
is nearest the bridge just mentioned.)

SIGNALS

My signal to you: One vertical mark of white adhesive tape meaning I am ready to receive your
package.

Your signal to me: One horizontal mark of white
adhesive tape meaning drop filled.

My signal to you: One vertical mark of white adhesive tape meaning I have received your
package.

(Remove old tape before leaving signal.)

I will acknowledge amount with my next package.

The KGB then loaded a package with $50,000 in cash and proposed in-
structions for future communications with their anonymous agent with the
extraordinary access. They would later receive a "thank you" note for the
money and an unusual suggestion for a future communications plan. The
KGB had suggested maintaining communications through the U.S. Postal system. But that plan was quickly rejected by the anonymous agent Cherkashin
and Degtyar were now referring to by the code names "KARAT" and "The
Source." Their anonymous friend, however, began referring to himself as "B."

Rather than continue taking what he considered at the beginning of his
operation as a "necessary risk," "B" offered a radically different, high-tech
mode of communications. The KGB was to use "a microcomputer bulletin
board" that "B" would designate and that would be protected by the "appropriate encryption" technology. "B" concluded his thank-you note as follows:

IF YOU WISH TO CONTINUE DISCUSSIONS, PLEASE HAVE
SOMONEONE RUN AN ADVERTISMENT IN THE
WASHINGTON TIMES DURING THE WEEK OF 1/12/87 OR
1/19/87, FOR SALE "DODGE DIPLOMAT, 1971, NEEDS
ENGINE WORK, $1000." GIVE A PHONE NUMBER AND
TIME OF DAY IN THE ADVERTISEMENT WHERE I CAN
CALL. I WILL CALL AND LEAVE A PHONE NUMBER
WHERE A RECORDED MESSAGE CAN BE LEFT FOR ME IN
ONE HOUR. THE NUMBER WILL BE IN THE AREA CODE
212. I WILL NOT SPECIFY THAT AREA CODE ON THE LINE.

Unlike Ames and Pollard, almost from the beginning of his treason "B" was keenly aware that printing and collecting too many documents pertaining to the compromise of recent high-profile Soviet double-agents would arouse suspicion. In fact, David Major, a former FBI supervisory special agent and the former director of counterintelligence at the National Security Council, would later characterize "B" as "diabolically brilliant" and a master spy.[62] "B's" understanding of the limits of his own access and the inner workings of the new computer-based intelligence community not only forced him to move ahead slowly but also forced him to begin planning for the end when he would ultimately be caught. "Nothing lasts forever," he wrote to his KGB handlers, adding "…I would appreciate an escape plan."

.. -. ... .. -.. . / .--- --- -...

For five days, starting on July 14, 1986, the Washington Times ran the following classified advertisement:

> DODGE – '71, DIPLOMAT, NEEDS ENGINE
> WORK, $1000. PHONE (703) 451-9780. (CALL
> NEXT MON., WED., FRI. 1 p.m.)

On Monday, July 21, the sound of a ringing telephone interrupted the low rumble of the busy Old Keene Mill Shopping Center near Burke, Virginia. Aleksandr Kirillovich Fefelov[63], a Washington-based KGB officer, walked through the light rain and the puddles on the ground to answer the ringing telephone. For a moment, there was no sound on the other end of the telephone. Rustling and crackling filled the handset now pressed firmly against Fefelov's right ear. Then, with confidence and precision, the person on the other end began to talk.

"Hello," he said. "My name is Ramon. I am calling about the car you offered for sale in the Times."

"I'm sorry," said Fefelov. "But the man with the car is not here. Can I get your number?

"628-8047."

.. -. ... .. -.. . / .--- --- -...

By 1987, Ramon had completed his second tour in New York and had returned to FBI headquarters. He purchased a new home on Talisman Drive in Vienna, Virginia. His regular communications with the KGB continued, as did their large cash payments for his services.

On a crisp November 23 of that year, Ramon left a package at a pre-determined dead drop site. Inside was a stack of valuable human intelligence debriefings from a Soviet defector and a technical document describing the inner workings of a system called COINS-II (Community Online Intelligence System). It was the U.S. intelligence community's classified intranet for sharing information. For this the KGB deposited $20,000 at the drop site and informed Ramon that $100,000 had been placed in an escrow account in Moscow in his name. They also promised him 6-7% interest on that investment.

By Feb. 1988, Ramon had shifted his communications from typed letters to floppy disks. During the next several months, Ramon delivered electronic copies of Top Secret documents pertaining to U.S. communications intelligence capabilities. The KGB became concerned, however, when they were unable to read some of the disks. Ramon informed them in a subsequent letter to "use 40 Track Mode," a reference to a technical procedure for re-formatting a computer disk while concealing the data stored in specific tracks on the disk. Unless the person trying to read the disk uses the correct codes to unlock (decrypt) the disk it appears to be unreadable.

Between Feb. 1988 and Dec. 1991, Ramon passed 26 floppy disks to the KGB detailing dozens of sensitive intelligence operations, sources and collection methods. He downloaded, printed and copied so much information, however, that the KGB actually wrote him a warning note: "Examine from the point of view of security your practice of copying materials."

Ramon agreed with the KGB's recommendation to find a "more secure" form of communication. And by June 2000, he had decided upon a new method. Ramon detailed his new plan to the KGB in the following letter:

> One of the commercial products currently available is the Palm VII Organizer. I have a Palm III, which is actually a fairly capable computer. The VII version comes with wireless Internet capability built in. It can allow the rapid transmission of encrypted messages, which if used on an infrequent basis, could be quite effective in preventing confusions if the existance [sic] of the accounts could be appropriately hidden as well as the existance [sic] of the devices themselves. Such a device might even serve for rapid transmittal of substantial material in digital form. Your FAPSI[64] could review what would be needed, its advisability, etc., obviously – particularly safe rules of use. While FAPSI may move with the rapidity of the Chinese army, they can be quite effective, in juggernaut fashion, that is to say thorough…

The following November, Ramon delivered the largest package of documents of his espionage career: nearly 1,000 photocopied pages downloaded from the FBI's Automated Case Support System.

Eventually, the FBI operation to uncover the Soviet source within the

U.S. intelligence community began closing in on Ramon. On Tuesday, Dec. 12, 2000, an FBI surveillance team staked out Foxstone Park on Creek Crossing Rd. in Vienna, Virginia – a known dead drop site for the KGB's ongoing operation handling Ramon. That evening, as the sun fell below the horizon and the temperature dropped into the 20s, a car drove by the park slowly, its occupant studying the Foxstone Park sign closely. It was obvious to the FBI agents that the driver was looking for a signal indicating that the KGB had made a cash drop for him to pick up. There was no signal present, so the car continued to move. Later that evening, FBI personnel watched as the same person who had suspiciously studied the Foxstone Park dead drop site entered a store at a nearby shopping center. A known Soviet foreign intelligence service agent stood quietly outside the store. It was more than a coincidence. And it was a shock to most officials inside the FBI that the suspicious person known to the Soviets as Ramon and the most damaging spy in the history of U.S. intelligence turned out to be one of their own – an insider.

.. -. ... .. -.. . / .--- --- -...

The spy known as "Ramon," "B," "KARAT," and "The Source," was actually Robert Phillip Hanssen, a career FBI agent who had worked his way up the corporate ladder at the Bureau to become the deputy chief of the FBI's Soviet Analysis unit.

During the next several weeks, FBI agents observed Hanssen checking for a signal at the Foxstone Park dead drop site no less than a dozen times. Then, on Feb. 12, 2001, the FBI team removed a package from the site and sent it to the FBI lab to be opened, analyzed and photocopied as evidence. It contained $50,000 in used one-hundred dollar bills and a note detailing the date of the next package exchange. The agents then placed the package back at the drop site and allowed Hanssen to pick it up.

The FBI soon applied for and was granted a court order to search Hanssen's office at FBI headquarters as well as his personal car. In addition to fingerprints linking him directly to the packages left at the drop site, the searches turned up electronic storage devices containing letters associated with "B," and seven classified documents that had been downloaded and printed from the FBI's Automated Case Support (ACS) system. Forensic analysis of Hanssen's Palm III handheld computer also revealed references to a particular dead drop site used by "B" and the KGB.

However, the FBI's most sobering discovery had to do with Hanssen's use of the Bureau's own IT infrastructure. To their dismay, the FBI found that Hanssen had used his authorized access to the Bureau's Automated Case Support system and his knowledge of computers to monitor the FBI investigation that was trying to find him.

At the heart of the ACS system, which first came online in 1995, is the

Electronic Case File (ECF). The ECF contains all of the Bureau's internal communications relating to ongoing investigations and programs.

Subsequent investigation of Hanssen's use of the ECF system showed that he routinely searched the system using search terms directly related to the investigation that was aimed at uncovering his identity. According to the affidavit filed in support of the criminal complaint against him, the FBI concluded that by searching the ECF database "Hanssen could retrieve certain FBI records that would indicate whether Hanssen or his KGB/SVR[65] associates, or their activities or operational locations, were known to or suspected by the FBI, and thus whether he was exposed to danger."[66] In fact, Hanssen conducted 35 searches of the ECF database during the span of his espionage activities. He often used search terms such as, "Hanssen, Dead Drop, Foxstone, KGB and Russia."[67]

The FBI arrested Robert Phillip Hanssen on Feb. 18, 2001 – more than 15 years after his first act of espionage. For his service, the KGB paid Hanssen more than $600,000 in cash and diamonds. Former KGB officer Victor Cherkashin characterized Hanssen's insider activity as more important to KGB espionage activities than that of Ames or any other mole. And that is no surprise. Hanssen comprised thousands of pages of classified documents detailing the most sensitive intelligence collection programs in the U.S. intelligence community. He also compromised the work of multiple human sources and the intelligence community's knowledge of Soviet military forces. Among the most damaging disclosures concerned the details of a tunnel that had been dug beneath the Soviet embassy in Washington and outfitted with high-tech listening devices that were monitored by the FBI and the NSA. "The information Hanssen provided Moscow," Cherkashin wrote in his memoir, "was worth tens of billions of dollars."[68]

.. -. ... .. -.. . / .--- --- -...

Robert Phillip Hanssen may have been a master spy, but he was not unique among insiders. This is especially true from a psychological perspective. Like Pollard and Ames, Hanssen seems to have been a troubled person. Although a self-described devout Christian, he is known to have secretly arranged to have a close associate watch as he had sex with his wife.

And like other high-tech insiders whom we will meet in the coming pages, Hanssen had a tendency to criticize and belittle the decisions of senior managers. He often spoke about the FBI's inability as an organization to function in a way that would help it succeed against the KGB and other foreign intelligence services. In fact, Hanssen was so disdainful of authority (particularly the lack of technical knowledge demonstrated by senior managers at the FBI) that he hacked into the computer of Ray Mislock, the former head of the national security section at the FBI Washington Field Office, just to prove that the system was not secure. He also installed a password-cracking program on his office computer while he was serving as FBI liaison to the State Department. When questioned about this at the time, Hanssen said that he had to reconfigure his FBI computer system at his State Department office to install a color printer. And because he could not do so without the password of a system administrator, who was rarely available to assist him, he broke the administrator's password and installed the printer himself.

From a social perspective, Hanssen was somewhat of an enigma. He seemed incapable of having a friendly conversation on a topic other than work. In fact, his peers at the bureau thought of him as a grim dullard. And like Pollard and Ames, Hanssen seems to have been able to overcome the natural inhibitions to criminal behavior by compartmentalizing his private life (where he was married to a devout member of the fundamentalist Opus Dei sect of the Catholic Church and a father of six children) from his life as a spy for a Communist system he denounced as "Godless."[69]

In August, 2003, the Office of the Inspector General at the Department of Justice issued a 674-page Top Secret report assessing the FBI's performance in unraveling Hanssen's espionage activities. And while the document does a good job of detailing Hanssen's activities and the information he compromised, it does not paint an accurate picture of Hanssen as a person or as a spy. The OIG report, for example, characterizes Hanssen as a "mediocre agent who exhibited strong technical skills but had weak managerial and interpersonal skills."[70] This conclusion has been incorrectly interpreted to mean that Hanssen was an unskilled spy – a conclusion that his chief Soviet handler flatly rejects.

The OIG report also points out that while Hanssen's daily activity did not overtly indicate that he was involved in espionage, a later evaluation of his performance did reveal that he had repeatedly mishandled classified information. More important, these security violations were ignored by his supervisors.

Unlike Pollard and Ames, however, Hanssen did not have a problem with alcohol or drugs, and did not engage in unbridled spending with the money he was receiving from the KGB. But the OIG report does outline several psychological factors that could partially explain his behavior and his willingness to engage in espionage. The report claims that as a boy Hanssen was abused emotionally by his father. Likewise, the report depicts Hanssen as a young man with an abnormal fascination with spies, going so far as to open a Swiss bank account. Hanssen joined the FBI with "serious personal insecurities, low self-esteem, and a fascination with espionage," none of which surfaced during his application process, the report states.[71]

Robert Hanssen, however, fit the mold of the typical introvert that psychology experts say are drawn to the information technology profession – a profession that often reinforces one's lack of interpersonal skills. During one of his tours in the New York Field Office, for example, Hanssen often took advantage of unrestricted and unmonitored access to the office's file room, where he spent hours reading Soviet espionage files that he had little or no "need to know" and that were outside the purview of his official duties at the time. Likewise, supervisors noted that he had little aptitude for field work (which requires highly developed interpersonal skills). Instead, he took every opportunity he could, even when those opportunities were the result of his own unauthorized access, to highlight his computer skills – skills that eventually put him "at the center of the information flow."[72]

At FBI headquarters, one of Hanssen's supervisors would comment that he was the "strangest person" he had ever met at the FBI – a "kind of cipher who was rigid, dour, and a religious zealot."[73] Those who worked under him later said they considered him distant and arrogant.

But while the psychological profile of Hanssen may indicate the potential for insider abuse, the fact remains that his espionage activities, which were marked by an insatiable appetite to view and print classified information, went undetected for more than a decade. The warning signals were there but the alarm never rang. And not once during the years that he spied for the Soviet Union was Robert Phillip Hanssen subjected to a polygraph examination or challenged about his excessive information consumption.

The ensuing government inquiry into the Hanssen spy case had profound ramifications throughout the FBI. On August 17, 2001, the Department of Justice asked William H. Webster, a former director of both the CIA and the FBI, to lead an independent commission to study what had gone wrong inside the FBI that could have enabled Hanssen to avoid detection for so long. The commission, known popularly as the Webster Commission, issued its detailed report on March 31, 2002.

In his letter to Attorney General John Ashcroft, Webster wrote of Hanssen: "He was proficient in combing FBI automated record systems, and he printed or downloaded to disk reams of highly classified information. Hanssen also did not hesitate to walk into Bureau units in which he had worked some time before, log on to stand-alone data systems, and retrieve, for example, the identities of foreign agents whom U.S. intelligence services had compromised, information vital to American interests and even more immediately vital to those whose identities Hanssen betrayed."[74]

The Webster report, however, held the FBI to account for the lax information system security that enabled Hanssen's espionage activities. "Bureau personnel routinely upload classified information into widely accessed databases, a form of electronic open storage that allows essentially unregulated downloading and printing," Webster wrote. "This practice once again violates the most basic security principle: only personnel with security clearances who need to know classified information to perform their duties should have access to that information. In spite of the practically unrestricted access many

Bureau employees have to information affecting national security, the FBI lags far behind other Intelligence Community agencies in developing information security countermeasures. For instance, an information system auditing program would surely have flagged Hanssen's frequent use of FBI computer systems to determine whether he was the subject of a counterintelligence investigation."[75]

At a press conference announcing the arrest of Hanssen, then FBI Director Louis Freeh said most, if not all, of the Bureau's information systems required detailed study to find ways to improve security and also to monitor for unusual behavior. However, "at the end of the day," said Freeh, "what we rely upon are honest people."

Robert Hanssen pled guilty to espionage charges on July 6, 2001. He was sentenced on May 10, 2002 to life imprisonment.

"Any clerk in the Bureau could come up with stuff on that system," Hanssen told the FBI during his post-arrest debriefing. "It was pathetic. . . It's criminal what's laid out. What I did is criminal, but it's criminal negligence . . . what they've done on that system," he added. "If they had been [monitoring computer use], I probably wouldn't have been making the kind of queries that I was making. So, it would have affected the way I used the machine. It may have prevented the disclosure of things."[76]

The Hanssen case, however, would not be the last example of the FBI's internal security problems. Despite the hard lessons that the Bureau learned from Hanssen and the steps undertaken to fix the internal security gaps that the master spy had taken advantage of, there would be others who would use their trusted access for both criminal and personal financial gain.

On July 17, 2003, for example, agents arrested 36-year-old Mario Castillo, an FBI language specialist with the Bureau's El Paso division. Castillo was charged in connection with three indictments outlining six counts of unauthorized access of a computer to obtain information for private financial gain and four counts of making a false statement to a federal official. The indictments, which are formal accusations of criminal conduct but not evidence of guilt,[77] allege that between July 13, 2000 to November 12, 2002, Castillo intentionally exceeded his authority and accessed an FBI computer on six different occasions for the purpose of private financial gain.

Prosecutors also allege that Castillo knowingly and willfully lied to federal agents when questioned about other paid employment and financial indebtedness, provided confidential information to unauthorized persons, and had ties and associations with a convicted felon. The second indictment charges Castillo with one count of trafficking in and using an unauthorized access device with intent to defraud. It alleges that from October 2002 to January 2003, Castillo collected more than $1,000 in money and goods as a result of his trafficking in and using stolen cellular telephones. The third indictment charges Castillo with one count of possession of child pornography, one count of receiving child pornography via the Internet and two counts of receipt of obscene material.

On May 9, 2003, FBI agents seized a computer from Castillo's residence. Subsequent forensic analysis of the contents stored on the computer revealed several video files and more than a dozen images containing obscene material, depicting minors engaged in sexually explicit conduct.

Another Texas-based FBI agent, Jeffrey D. Fudge, was indicted on Nov. 5, 2003 on various felony charges related to the misuse of his position of trust as an FBI employee with access to sensitive computer systems and information.

As an investigative analyst, Fudge's duties included conducting database searches using the FBI's internal network, serving subpoenas, analyzing telephone records, and providing general assistance to FBI agents who were conducting criminal and administrative investigations. To do his job, Fudge was granted access to databases related to the FBI Automated Case Support system (ACS), the National Crime Information Center (NCIC), the Texas Crime Information Center (TCIC), the Texas Law Enforcement Telecommunications System (TLETS), and the FBI Network (FBINET). He was authorized to access FBI computers and FBI computer systems and programs only for official business and "need to know."

According to the indictment, however, from October 7, 1997 through April 25, 2003, Fudge accessed FBI files and disclosed information from the files to friends and family members. He also accessed the FBI's computer system to determine if the FBI was investigating particular individuals, including several locally-prominent citizens. Likewise, he accessed FBI files to satisfy his own curiosity about FBI investigations. As of this writing, there is no word on whether Fudge has been found guilty or innocent.

.. -. ... .. -.. . / .--- --- -...

Believe it or not, at a time when American nationalism is at its highest levels in decades – one might even argue at dangerous levels – the nation still has insiders to deal with who are motivated by ideological reasons. The example of Ana Belen Montes, a senior intelligence analyst at the Defense Intelligence Agency (DIA) who was arrested on Sept. 21, 2001 for spying on behalf of Cuba, is a perfect example.

Montes served as the DIA's senior analyst for Cuban matters. But she led a double life. An unmarried loner who lived in an apartment on Macomb Street in Northwest Washington, D.C., Montes was considered a rising star within the DIA bureaucracy. She saved her money, kept an immaculate apartment, went to the gym on a regular basis, and was the epitome of the typical American upbringing. But by Sept. 2001 — nine years after first specializing in Cuban intelligence matters — Montes had also become the most important spy ever to work for the Cuban government.

But there were clues that the unflappable, respectful and punctual Ana Belen Montes was living another life in parallel to her official life at the DIA. She sometimes went on vacations alone to exotic locations, and would probably have had a hard time explaining (if anybody had noticed) her repeated visits to public pay phones around the Washington, D.C., area. And had anybody walked in on Ana at her apartment in the wee hours of the morning, she likely would have found it difficult to explain the presence of a Sony shortwave radio and the sounds of encrypted messages emanating from the earpiece.

The Cuban intelligence service routinely communicates with its clandestine agents abroad using shortwave radio. A series of numbers are broadcasted using a high-frequency communications channel. Agents then pick up those numbers using their shortwave radios and enter them into a laptop computer. They then insert a floppy disk or CD-ROM that contains a program that converts what appears to be a random series of numbers into Spanish language text. This was the same method of communication that FBI officials uncovered when they broke up a Cuban spy ring based in Florida -- known as the Wasp Network -- that attempted to infiltrate Cuban exile organizations and U.S. military installations.

Although they ultimately failed to avoid detection, Montes and her Cuban handlers were keenly aware of the risk posed by excessive information access. As a result, Montes' handlers instructed her to keep only the information that was reasonable for her to have access to at any one time. She also made a habit of transmitting information derived from direct conversations and meetings, avoiding excessive downloading and printing of data.

For example, Montes transmitted details of meetings she attended at which the identity of a U.S. intelligence agent who was about to travel to Cuba was discussed. Her handlers thanked her for the information, saying they were waiting "for him with open arms."

She also divulged information about a military exercise hosted by the U.S. Atlantic Command (ACOM) that she was scheduled to take part in. ACOM is the U.S. military command responsible for the Cuba area of operations and for developing military contingency plans concerning Cuba. "Practically, everything that takes place there will be of intelligence value," Montes' handlers wrote.[78] "Let's see if it deals with contingency plans and specific targets in Cuba, which are [priority] interests for us." And, of course, that exercise and others like it was of great interest to Cuba, particularly the operators manning the Lourdes listening post.

Built by the Russians near the abandoned village of Lourdes, the facility's value today is increasingly a topic of debate among intelligence experts. But during the time of Montes' espionage activities, Lourdes was clearly a valuable asset in the Russian intelligence arsenal. In fact, it was and remains the only major electronic intercept capability that the Russian FAPSI can rely upon to directly target U.S. communications. And in 1996, it did that relatively well.

At the time of Montes' spying activities, the Lourdes facility was capable of intercepting the bulk of telephone communications along the Eastern seaboard of the United States. U.S. voice and data telephone transmissions relayed by satellite were also highly vulnerable to systematic interception. Personal information about U.S. citizens in the private and government sectors could be picked out of the airwaves and used to blackmail potential espionage recruits.

As with Aldrich Ames, Montes' espionage activities were enabled by her access and senior position within the DIA. However, she also took the extraordinary step of refusing a promotion as a means to maintain her access to Cuban intelligence matters — perhaps the only major red flag in this case.

Unlike some of the previous cases we have looked at, Montes appears to be an example of an insider who was motivated by ideology. This is interesting given that many believed ideologically-based espionage had given way to personal financial motivations or delusions of grandeur. The following is the statement issued by Ana Belen Montes after her conviction and sentencing to 25 years in prison on October 16, 2002:

> "An Italian proverb perhaps best describes the fundamental truth I believe in: `All the world is one country.' In such a 'world-country,' the principle of loving one's neighbor as much as oneself seems, to me, to be the essential guide to harmonious relations between all of our "nation-neighborhoods." This principle urges tolerance and understanding for the different ways of others. It asks that we treat other nations the way we wish to be treated -- with respect and compassion. It is a principle that, tragically, I believe we have never applied to Cuba.

> Your honor, I engaged in the activity that brought me before you because I obeyed my conscience rather than the law. I believe our government's policy towards Cuba is cruel and unfair, profoundly un-neighborly, and I felt morally obligated to help the island defend itself from our efforts to impose our values and our political system on it. We have displayed intolerance and contempt towards Cuba for most of the last four decades. We have never respected Cuba's right to make its own journey towards its own ideals of equality and justice. I do not understand why we must continue to dictate how the Cubans should select their leaders, who their leaders cannot be, and what laws are appropriate in their land. Why can't we let Cuba pursue its own internal journey, as the United States has been doing for over two centuries?

> My way of responding to our Cuba policy may have been morally wrong. Perhaps Cuba's right to exist free of political and economic

coercion did not justify giving the island classified information to help it defend itself. I can only say that I did what I thought right to counter a grave injustice.

My greatest desire is to see amicable relations emerge between the United States and Cuba. I hope my case in some way will encourage our government to abandon its hostility towards Cuba and to work with Havana in a spirit of tolerance, mutual respect, and understanding. Today we see more clearly than ever that intolerance and hatred -- by individuals or governments -- spread only pain and suffering. I hope for a U.S. policy that is based instead on neighborly love, a policy that recognizes that Cuba, like any nation, wants to be treated with dignity and not with contempt. Such a policy would bring our government back in harmony with the compassion and generosity of the American people. It would allow Cubans and Americans to learn from and share with each other. It would enable Cuba to drop its defensive measures and experiment more easily with changes. And it would permit the two neighbors to work together and with other nations to promote tolerance and cooperation in our one 'world-country,' in our only 'world-homeland.'"

To many, Montes' vision of a "one world-country in our only world-homeland" may seem like the dream of a whimsical, idealistic personality. But again, it is not these beliefs alone that should raise our suspicions. As with other "at risk" groups, we must find a balance between such personal beliefs and the point at which personal beliefs are shifted into potentially malicious or criminal behavior. In Montes' case, this was extremely difficult to do.

Montes' insider activity once took the form of malicious omission of facts — an extremely difficult security breach to pick up on and perhaps even beyond any technical capability to uncover. In early 1998, Montes wrote an executive intelligence briefing on the threat posed by Cuba's military to U.S. national security interests. The briefing was to be used by then Secretary of Defense William Cohen. To Cohen's surprise, however, the briefing painted a picture of a Cuba almost completely devoid of hostile intent against the U.S. and with little or no involvement in the international arms market. Cohen was so surprised by this that he actually added sections to the report that underscored Cuba's potential to develop dangerous offensive biological weapons.

In this sense, Montes was among the most dangerous of insider spies. She was in a position to slowly and gently influence major policy decisions to support the intelligence goals of those she worked for. In addition, unlike her money-hungry predecessors, Montes did not ask for compensation and, therefore, left no telltale signs that she was a spy. And perhaps most important, she was motivated by a desire to right a perceived wrong. Ana Belen Montes may have been the last of the ideological spies of the 20th century, if not one of the most difficult to understand. Shortly after the terrorist attacks of Sept. 11, 2001, a neighbor sent Montes an e-mail and got an unusually emotional response. "Right now, I'm not in the mood to talk," she wrote, adding that she was grief-stricken due to the attacks.[79]

There will almost certainly be others who will follow in Montes' steps. And as a result, we must be ever-vigilant not to become consumed with and distracted by the current espionage flavor of the day: financial gain and economic intelligence.

.. -. ... .. -.. . / .--- --- -...

Recent insider risk assessments conducted by Reconnex Corp. have revealed that malicious insiders and misuse of computer networks remain major threats to the government. The cases of insider espionage and criminal activity highlighted thus far are only representative of the high-profile cases in which the perpetrator was caught. The 48-hour risk assessments conducted by Reconnex, on the other hand, show a problem that is growing in both its breadth and level of danger.

At one agency, which employs tens of thousands of people, the Reconnex team conducted two 48-hour risk assessments to satisfy the questions of the agency's leadership. During the first assessment in early April 2005, the Reconnex iGuard system noted more than 700 instances of social security numbers and four instances of credit card numbers leaving the network unencrypted and being sent to unknown locations on the Internet. Likewise, at least 11 engineering documents and more than 4,445 documents containing software source code were recorded leaving the agency's network.

The second risk assessment, conducted in May, revealed even more problems at the agency. An additional 209 e-mails and Web postings were discovered containing more than 2,000 social security numbers. Other, non-work related findings (and major legal liabilities) included 169 pornographic Web pages, 4,372 hate and racist Web pages, 1,005 gambling sites, and 58,405 shopping Web pages.

During a two-week long assessment conducted at another major federal agency between October 19, 2004 and November 3, 2004, many of the same problems were noted—credit card numbers, social security numbers and multiple instances of proprietary source code left the network via unencrypted e-mail and various Web postings.

"Beyond concerns of intellectual property are the security risks surrounding this leak," the Reconnex risk assessment states. "If this is source code to key systems, this could give hackers a 'look under the covers' of the system and allow them easier access into the system, which could represent a serious national security threat." Additionally, this could also be a violation of the

Federal Information Security Management Act (FISMA), which requires federal agencies to develop, maintain and review security controls to protect government information and systems.

At least one government agency was the unfortunate recipient of e-mails and other in-bound communications that contained social security numbers. In this particular case, the unencrypted and vulnerable communications originated within organizations in Illinois and Nebraska, as well as Richland and Lake Land Community Colleges in Illinois.

One particular federal agency that is well aware of the legal implications of electronic privacy violations was quite surprised at the results of a week-long risk assessment conducted in April 2005. Dozens of the agency's users were responsible for e-mailing at least 147 social security numbers in clear text during the assessment period. In addition, there were more than a half-million images (JPEGs and GIFs) flying across the network during that week. At least three engineering documents and 56 source code files also left the network in the clear.

The results of three other government risk assessments were just as troubling.

Assessment
Length of Assessment: 1 Week

Social Security Numbers Discovered: 257 in clear text
Credit Cards: 8

Image files:
JPEG: 255,758
GIF: 228, 279
BMP: 716
TIFF 10
PNG: 2,390

Unencrypted Source Code Leaving Network: 6 languages, 94 instances

Assessment
Length of Assessment: 48 hours

Social Security Numbers Discovered: 13 in clear text
Credit Cards: 0

Image Files:
7,400 GIFs
4,800 JPEGs

16,000 WAVE files also noted
2,600 Shockwave files noted

Unencrypted Source Code Leaving Network: 9 languages, more than 900 instances
Unencrypted Engineering Documents Leaving Network: 80

Assessment
Length of Assessment: 48 hours (results discovered in 3 hours of forensic
evaluation)
Social Security Numbers Discovered in Documents: 92
Social Security Numbers Discovered in Outbound Messages: 22
Private Health Information Discovered in Outbound Communications: 16
Pornographic Images: 6 (More than 200 pornographic e-mails noted from a
single user)
Outbound Usernames and Passwords in Messages: 4
Source code on Non-Standard Ports: 4

Other findings: Possible SPAM relay infection was noted on the agency's
network. In addition, one Social Security Number hit included complete
money wiring instructions, including name, address, date of birth, and bank
account number.

.. -. ... .. -.. . / .--- --- -...

There is more to the government insider story, however. In fact, the findings of a Reconnex risk assessment at a major government agency support
Jerrold Post's workplace violence (and ID theft as a species of assassination)
analogy. This particular risk assessment uncovered dozens of pieces of evidence containing hate speech and images. "It was so bad," said Daniel Smith,
Reconnex's risk-assessment leader, "that the officials who were present during the review of the data had to either turn their heads or leave the room."

News Story

Ex-Teledata employee pleads guilty in massive ID theft case

He was involved in a bid to steal the identities of up to 30,000 people

News Story by Linda Rosencrance

SEPTEMBER 15, 2004 (COMPUTERWORLD) - A former help desk employee at Teledata Communications Inc. pleaded guilty yesterday in a massive scheme to steal the identities of up to 30,000 people, according to U.S. Attorney David Kelley.

Teledata provides banks and other entities with computerized access to consumer credit reports from the three commercial credit history bureaus -- Equifax Inc., Experian Information Solutions Inc. and Trans Union LLC.

Cartersville, Ga., resident Philip Cummings, 34, pleaded guilty to one count of conspiracy, one count of wire fraud and one count of fraud in connection with the case, Kelley said in a statement. Cummings had been scheduled to go on trial Nov. 3.

The lead defendant in the largest identity theft case known to U.S. authorities, Cummings faces a combined maximum sentence of 50 years in prison, according to Kelley. As part of his guilty plea, Cummings has agreed to forfeit any proceeds of the scheme, and is scheduled to be sentenced on Jan. 11.

According to the indictment, as a help desk worker at Hauppauge, N.Y.-based Teledata, Cummings had access to confidential passwords and subscriber codes of Teledata customers who used the company's software to download consumer credit histories from the credit bureaus for legitimate business needs.

From early 2000 through October 2002, Cummings and accused co-conspirator Linus Baptiste accessed the credit bureaus and downloaded more than 30,000 consumer credit reports, authorities said.

The indictment alleged that Baptiste then gave the stolen credit reports to a number of people, including co-defendant Eniete Ukpong, who is accused of using them to obtain, among other things, credit cards in the names of the various individuals listed in the reports. The trio would then allegedly use the credit cards to purchase merchandise, such as computers and electronic equipment, which was then resold to others, including co-defendant Ahmet Ulutas, Kelley said.

Ukpong and Ulutas are scheduled to go to trial on Nov. 3. Kelley said the investigation is continuing.

PART II

THE INSIDER IMPACT

News Story

Ameritrade warns 200,000 clients about potential data breach

A backup tape with account information is missing

News Story by Todd R. Weiss

APRIL 20, 2005 (COMPUTERWORLD) - A computer backup tape containing account information of more than 200,000 Ameritrade Inc. clients was apparently lost or accidentally destroyed while being shipped, prompting the online investment brokerage to notify the clients of a potential breach.

Donna Kush, a spokeswoman for the Omaha-based company, today confirmed that a package of data backup tapes was damaged in transit in late February by a shipping company that isn't being named. Four of the tapes in the package disappeared after the package was damaged but three were later found by the shipper during a search of its facility, she said.

The fourth tape is still missing and is presumed to still be lost in the facility or to have been destroyed accidentally.

"We do believe that foul play was not involved," Kush said. "We don't feel that any of the [client] information has led to any misuse." The backup tapes held account information for clients and former clients from 2001 to 2003, Kush said.

Last week, the clients began receiving letters from Ameritrade telling them of the incident and offering one free year of credit-protection services from Identity Track. Chantilly, Va.-based Identity Track monitors credit profiles and alerts clients to activity that may indicate identity theft -- including recent inquiries, new accounts or address changes. Consumers can also access and review their credit reports.

In its letter to clients, Ameritrade said it's adding another layer of security to their accounts.

Kush wouldn't discuss what is being done in detail. "We're evaluating our processes and procedures on what we do here and are making some changes," she said.

Kush said the company acted as quickly as possible after learning in late February that the tapes were missing. "It took some time to work with the [shipping] vendor" after the loss was discovered, she said. "It took some time just to find those three tapes." More time elapsed as the search continued for the fourth tape.

"We feel we acted promptly," she said.

The backup tapes weren't labeled with Ameritrade's name or logo or any other identifiable information, Kush said. Although the data on the tapes was compressed and special equipment would be needed to read it, the information wasn't encrypted.

Under California law, which mandates that customers be told of potential data breaches, the company would have been required to notify about 175,000 of the affected former and current clients. But Ameritrade chose to send letters to all potentially affected clients.

The incident differs from several other recent high-profile data loss cases, which largely involved computer system break-ins or the thefts of actual computers. Last week, about 106,000 alumni of Tufts University in Boston were notified that personal information stored on a server used by the university for fund raising could have been exposed to intruders.

Last month, officials at the University of California, Berkeley, said they were notifying more than 98,000 graduate students and applicants about the theft of a laptop computer on campus containing their names, Social Security numbers and other personal information. Another data breach that came to light in March involved data broker LexisNexis Group, which last week acknowledged that the personal information of some 310,000 people may have been exposed. And in an incident that became public in February, credit and personal information vendor ChoicePoint Inc. sold personal information on about 145,000 people to thieves posing as legitimate businesses.

Chapter 7

Identity Thieves

"Most insiders were motivated by financial gain, rather than a desire to harm the company or information system. Other motives included revenge, dissatisfaction with company management, culture or polices, and a desire for respect."
— U.S. Secret Service Insider Threat Study, August 2004[80]

T he infamous outlaw Jesse James likely spins in his grave each time somebody utters the following statistic: bank robberies are actually on the decline, with banks reporting only $70 million in losses in 2001 from robberies and average losses from those robberies totaling less than $5,000 per incident between 1996 and 2001. The decline of traditional-style bank robberies is a direct result of improvements in technology and the application of those technologies to the new banking environment. Today, banks are open, airy places, well-lighted and equipped with silent alarms, networked surveillance cameras, tainted "bait money" that enables law enforcement officers to track the thieves that manage to get away, and a massive electronic infrastructure that no longer requires bank tellers to have access to large stores of cash to conduct financial transactions.

But have bank robberies really declined in recent years? The answer to that question really depends on how you define bank robbery. In the modern age of electronic banking, Internet technologies have transformed the banking experience to such a significant degree that the concept of bank robbery can no longer be defined as its traditional form. Today, the traditional bank robbery, in which an armed robber physically enters a bank to carry out a "a stick-up," has been replaced by a growing multitude of fraud schemes, including check fraud, credit card fraud, automated clearing house (ACH) fraud, Internet commerce fraud, phishing scams, loan fraud, securities fraud, embezzlement, and identity theft.

The modern American bank has recognized the security risks associated with the new electronic frontier and, as a result, has deployed all the state-of-the-art electronic security devices that one would expect to find in a security-conscious enterprise – firewalls, intrusion detection devices, password management systems, and powerful encryption technologies. Yet banks and financial institutions continue to lose millions of dollars every year to trusted insiders who understand where the weaknesses are in the system.

In fact, insiders accounted for approximately 70%, or $2.4 billion, of the $3.4 billion that banks lost as a result of both internal and external fraud and hacker incidents in 2004. During the previous year, 24% of all FBI investigations and eventual convictions were related to insider fraud. In 2003, the FBI investigated nearly 7,300 cases of insider fraud in the banking and finance sector. Those investigations led to 2,397 convictions or pretrial diversions, leaving a whopping two-thirds of all reported cases unsolved.[81]

The FBI has also been tracking so-called "problem institutions" throughout the banking and finance industry. These organizations are defined as having "financial, operational or managerial weaknesses" that threaten their continued viability.

Following the deregulation of the savings and loan industry in 1982, the FBI initiated criminal investigations of hundreds of failed financial institutions throughout the United States. And while the number of investigations into failed financial institutions has declined steadily over the years, the total number of pending financial fraud and major case investigations continues to exceed levels at the beginning of the savings and loan crisis.

The FBI managed to produce 1,728 financial fraud convictions during fiscal 2004. More interesting, however, is the fact that nearly 1 out of every 5 individuals convicted of financial institution fraud was an insider of one type or another. The following chart depicts the types of individuals convicted in financial fraud cases during 2004.

SUBJECT TYPE	NUMBER OF SUBJECTS
All Other Subjects	1371
Bank Employee	283
Bank Officer	91
Illegal Alien	29
Legal Alien	18
Company or Corporation	11
Business Manager	3
Top Con Man	2
Boss	1

Federal Employee - GS 12 & Below	1
Federal Law Enforcement Officer	1
International or National Union Officer	1
Office Manager	1

CHART: Types of individuals convicted in financial fraud cases during 2004.

Security experts have also been tracking the confluence of organized criminal syndicates and insider abuse cases throughout the financial industry. While it has been difficult to prove, there is a considerable amount of anecdotal evidence that suggests organized criminal gangs have made an effort to plant people inside financial institutions for the purpose of stealing customer identity information that can then be sold on the black market. That market often takes the form of Web sites that offer "dumps" of hundreds and sometimes thousands of credit card numbers for a fee. Fees are often collected using various forms of electronic currency, such as Webmoney and E-gold. And for those who are extremely paranoid about being tracked down, some of these illegal data merchants accept "cash in a bag" as payment.

Some estimate the value of basic customer data to be approximately $5 per customer. However, a small electronic storage device holding information on tens of thousands of individuals can easily earn an insider several million dollars.

The FBI reported that between fiscal years 2002 and 2004 it "disrupted" 66 organized criminal gangs involved in financial institution fraud and "dismantled" 44 such enterprises. One such dismantlement operation, code-named "Operation Continued Action," took place on Sept. 17, 2004. It was among the largest nationwide enforcement operations in FBI history directed at organized groups and individuals engaged in financial institution fraud. Operation Continued Action involved 47 FBI Field Offices, covered a 30-day period and identified more than 271 subjects in 158 investigations. More than 151 indictments and complaints were filed, leading to more than 144 arrests, convictions, sentences, and millions of dollars in forfeiture and restitution. Estimates put the potential losses due to these fraud cases in excess of $3 billion.

.. -. ... .. -.. . / .--- --- -...

There is no better example of the confluence of organized crime and insider abuse in the finance and banking industry than the April 2005 theft of more than 675,000 identities in New Jersey.

The crime ring, led by Orazio Lembo of Hackensack, New Jersey, allegedly set up a front company called DRL Associates that masqueraded as a collection agency. Lembo then hired seven bank employees, including branch managers from Wachovia Corp., Bank of America Corp., Commerce Bancorp Inc., PNC Bank NA, and a former New Jersey Department of Labor manager to steal personal account data. The co-conspirators would pull up the data, including names and social security numbers that belonged to bank customers, and would either print the data out or copy it by hand. They then built a manual database of 675,000 identities and sold the data to more than 40 other collection agencies.

Federal and state law enforcement officials said the bank employees would normally conduct 40 to 50 searches of customer bank accounts as part of their daily, authorized job functions. During the time they were supporting the criminal endeavor of the identity theft ring, however, they allegedly performed up to 500 account searches a day, looking for new identities to steal.

Hackensack police investigators said Lembo paid the bank employees $10 for every record they delivered to him. He then charged the collection agencies between $70 and $100 per record. Lembo devised a separate arrangement with the New Jersey state Department of Labor official, who provided him with job and salary information on New Jersey residents. By combining the job data with the bank account information, Lembo was able to charge the collection agencies as much as $150 for the data. The identity scam earned Lembo as much as $4 million.

.. -. ... .. -.. . / .--- --- -...

New laws and regulations passed during the last few years in the wake of massive identity thefts and corporate accounting scandals have raised the security ante for corporate executives at all public corporations.

The Gramm-Leach-Bliley Act (GLBA) of 1999, for example, requires financial institutions, including insurance entities, to protect the confidentiality of their customers' personal information and ensure that it is secure during transfer and collection. The GLBA also requires regulators, including state insurance regulators, to enforce these protections.

The Sarbanes-Oxley Act of 2002, for example, was designed to eliminate the ability of executives to illegally "cook the books" by inflating stock prices and filing misleading or false financial statements. And with virtually all financial data being controlled and managed electronically, the risks of insider abuse or sabotage is significant.

This was evident to many in the aftermath of the firing of Kenneth Livesay from his position as the chief information officer (CIO) at HealthSouth Corp. in Birmingham, Ala. The case against Livesay, who pled guilty in federal court in 2003 to falsifying the company's earnings and financial statements, highlighted the impact that new laws such as Sarbanes-Oxley are having on IT operations. Suddenly, it became imperative that IT security controls be sufficient to prevent such abuses from happening. Internal control of the corporate enterprise was no longer the sole responsibility of the CEO and CFO (chief financial officer), but of every officer of the company – including the officer responsible for the electronic infrastructure, the CIO.

The third law to make up the 'big three' potential legal nightmares for companies is California's S.B. 1386 privacy statute. The law, which went into effect on July 1, 2003, requires companies that do business with California residents (regardless of where the companies are located in the U.S.) to inform customers when their names, in combination with personal identification information, have been accessed by an unauthorized person.

When one considers the type and frequency of internal security breaches that are taking place throughout the public and private sectors in America, the implications of these laws are profound.

.. -. ... .. -.. . / .--- --- -...

Malicious insider activity in the banking and finance sector takes many different forms. It can involve everyone from low-level clerks to senior vice presidents and other corporate officers. Likewise, it can involve outside entities, such as organized crime rings, working in tandem with unscrupulous insiders.

For example, in October 2003, Jean Pierre "Johnny" Harper pled guilty to one count of conspiracy to commit bank fraud and bribery. A former vice president at the Birmingham, Alabama–based Compass Bank, Harper was convicted of defrauding the bank of $10 million by accepting bribes from what the FBI called "questionable" telemarketers to process credit card charges at the bank's processing center. Although these telemarketers had been banned by credit card companies, Harper allowed them to open accounts with his employer using false identities. He allegedly ran the inside operation for almost a year before his employer became aware that the accounts were actually owned by telemarketers. Prosecutors likened the case to a situation in which a trusted insider leaves the bank door open after hours so that thieves can easily gain access. Before Interpol agents arrested him in Costa Rica, Harper led them on a long and arduous 8-month search that included tips from France, Canada, Lebanon and St. Croix.

On February 27, 2004, authorities succeeded in obtaining a guilty plea to one count of bank fraud from Mark Kovack, a former vice president, branch manager and loan officer at First Midwest Bank, a division of Jacksonville Savings Bank based in Virden, Illinois. The indictment returned in the Kovack case alleged that he converted bank funds to his personal use and used fraudulent transactions to make payments on uncollectible or marginally collectible loans he had previously made. Kovack's fraudulent transactions included diverting or misapplying payments by creditworthy customers which were intended to be applied to their loans or accounts; diverting or misapplying advances made from construction loans that Kovack made without the knowledge of the construction loan customers; and taking out loans in the names of customers who had no knowledge of the creation of such loans.

During a court appearance on Feb. 27, 2004, Kovack admitted that he concealed his activities by making loan payments using incoming payments belonging to customers. Kovack admitted he would similarly divert and misapply funds from other accounts to conceal his fraudulent transactions. In addition, when some customers with bad loans authorized by Kovack filed for bankruptcy, Kovack would deliberately fail to promptly notify the banks of the action, causing them to lose substantial money because they failed to protect their interests in those proceedings. On Feb. 1, 2005, the Federal Deposit Insurance Corp. (FDIC) officially banned Kovack from participating in any manner in the day-to-day operations of any financial institution in the U.S.

But one of the best examples of IT insider activity in the banking and finance sector took place in March 2000 in lower Manhattan.

The company Internet Trading Technologies Inc. (ITTI), a New York-based technology subsidiary of stock trade regulator LaBranche & Co., had just completed a second round of funding that helped fuel a major expansion of the company's IT staff. Within two months of completing that round of funding, CEO Craig Goldberg hired six more software developers and tapped a CIO with 15 years of experience to take on the role of chief operating officer. Business was looking good for the firm, which processes a large amount of stock trades on the NASDAQ stock exchange.

But a malevolent force lurked beneath the surface at ITTI. It was a force that would not only attempt to blackmail the company out of millions of dollars, but in the process would take the firm to the edge of bankruptcy. Two of the company's software developers approached ITTI's new COO and demanded that the company "pay them a lot of money or they will resign immediately and not provide any assistance to the development team," according to details Goldberg provided to the author in an interview in July 2001. In a good faith effort to keep his employees happy, Goldberg offered one of the programmers, Abdelkader Smires, a $70,000 cash bonus and $50,000 in stock options.

But that wasn't enough for Smires and his alleged accomplice. Without warning, they stormed off the premises, demanding more money and stock options and threatening to let the firm's new, critical development work founder.

"It felt like we were being held up," Goldberg recalled. Faced with the equivalent of a cyber-hijacking, Goldberg refused to budge, and the developers were dismissed. And that's when trouble started – serious trouble.

The first denial-of-service attack struck the ITTI network the next morning, a Thursday, and crashed the company's application server. Somebody sitting at a computer in a downtown Manhattan Kinko's had gained access to ITTI's server using an internal development password. The server was brought back online, only to be cut off from the Internet again two minutes later. Passwords were changed, and development systems were air-gapped—physically disconnected—from the Internet. But the attacks continued through the weekend. The situation soon became critical.

"If the attacks continued to go on, we would go out of business," Goldberg recalled. He called in a security consulting firm and the U.S. Secret Service.

The last attack, which occurred Monday morning, occurred as federal authorities from the U.S. Secret Service Electronic Crimes Task Force were installing monitoring equipment on ITTI's networks. Authorities traced the attacker to a computer at Queens College in Flushing, N.Y., where Smires was a student. Witnesses placed the individual at the specific computer at the precise time of the attack. Within an hour, the Secret Service had their man. No evidence or charges were brought against the other former employee.

.. -. ... .. -.. . / .--- --- -...

The following are other notable insider cases involving embezzlement or financial fraud throughout the private sector:

Case: Insider Embezzlement.

David Alan Wolf was employed by the Beverly Hills Bar Association (BHBA) as its Controller/Director of Administration. Wolf embezzled funds by making checks payable to himself and depositing them into his account. Wolf forged signatures on the checks or deceived other employees into signing them, as Wolf did not have signatory authority on the account. On occasion, he would embezzle checks that had been pre-signed by an employee that was going out of town. Wolf utilized the funds to feed a gambling habit. The total amount embezzled was approximately $800,000. On June 16, 2004, Wolf plead guilty to three counts of Forgery of a Security. He was sentenced on August 30, 2004 to 33 months in prison.

Case: Insider Embezzlement.

On the same day that Wolf was pleading guilty to forgery of a security, Cynthia Reynolds pled guilty to one count of Embezzlement and one count of Criminal Forfeiture, before U.S. Magistrate Judge Jan Adler in the Southern District of California. Cynthia Reynolds was an employee of North Island Financial Credit Union (NIFCU).

As part of her responsibilities, she was authorized to move funds in and out of the NIFCU real estate suspense account. Reynolds embezzled at least $917,713 from that account by transferring money from the suspense account into a relative's account at NIFCU. Reynolds also generated official NIFCU checks drawn on the suspense account and improperly used the checks to purchase vehicles and pay various individuals and businesses for her and her relatives' benefit. Reynolds concealed her activity by making false entries into NIFCU's general ledger system. Her plea agreement forced her to quit-claim her residence to the North Island Financial Credit Union (NIFCU), as funds from the fraud had been used to pay for the residence.

Case: Insider Fraud.

On Sept. 13, 2004, Randy McArthur, a teller supervisor at the Bank of Ephraim in Ephraim, Utah, and his associate, Dean Johnson, entered guilty pleas to bank fraud charges for their alleged roles in a $5 million embezzlement scheme that contributed to the failure of the bank. This embezzlement took place over a 20-year period.

Case: Insider Fraud, Conspiracy.

On the following day, Philip J. Cummings, a former technical support representative at Telecommunications Data, Inc., pled guilty in a U.S. District Court in the Southern District of New York, to one count of Wire Fraud, one count of Fraud Related to Identification Documents and Information and one count of Conspiracy, for his participation in a massive scheme to steal the identities of individuals, which defrauded financial institutions of more than $11 million. It was alleged that Cummings stole the passwords and access codes of Ford Motor Credit and other financial companies, to access Equifax, Trans Union, and Experian credit report records and downloaded credit report information on 30,000 individuals. These credit reports were allegedly sold to a group of co-conspirators. To date, this is one of the largest identity theft cases in history.

Case: Insider Embezzlement.

On Sept. 15, 2004, Barbara Jane Coward was indicted for an embezzlement scheme targeting the Utah Copper Employee's Credit Union (UCECU). Coward was employed as the manager of the UCECU, where she had worked for 54 years. She allegedly embezzled $2.4 million from UCECU during a 40-year period, through the creation of fictitious loans.

Case: Insider Fraud.

As of this writing, Gary D. Jones, a former Wells Fargo business banker, is awaiting sentencing after pleading guilty to defrauding Wells and Capitol Credit Union of more than $1.3 million in cash and assets for personal use, including the funding of the NASCAR Busch series racing venture. Between 2000 and 2003, Jones used fake documents to create an identity and tap fraudulent loans.

Case: Insider Embezzlement.

In 2002, seven GTE managers were found guilty of embezzling $1.3 million from the company during a six-year period starting in 1992. Prosecutors alleged that the men submitted false expense reports and invoices from a fictional contracting company.

Case: Insider Embezzlement.

A former executive of the American Cancer Society admitted to and was found guilty of stealing more than $7 million from the organization. Daniel Wiant, the former executive, said he used his trusted position as a computer expert and chief financial officer to transfer the money to an overseas bank account.

Case: Insider Embezzlement.

In August 2002, Carol Watson, a former controller for Watson Coatings Inc., a manufacturer of industrial paints and coatings, pled guilty to embezzling $1.8 million from the company over a seven-year period. She used the company's funds to pay her personal credit card bills. The company was forced to lay off 11 employees and almost had to close its doors for good as a result of Watson's theft.

Employee theft and embezzlement is often the work of a lone perpetrator, such as an individual who cheats on an expense report, steals from a cash register or deliberately fails to record purchases for the purpose of pocketing the money for a product. However, recent studies have shown that widespread employee embezzlement can influence others to take part in the crime. A group social dynamic takes form, in which several employees devise schemes that directly benefit themselves while not causing catastrophic harm to the business. Some estimates place the financial damage stemming from employee theft and embezzlement, particularly as it relates to the loss of intellectual property, at upwards of $240 billion per year. This makes employees two to three times more costly to businesses than most other types of criminals combined.[82]

Women also hold a special place in the annals of fraud. According to Sandy Haantz, a research assistant with the National White Collar Crime Center, fraud felonies perpetrated by women jumped by 55% between 1990 and 1996. And by 1996, women accounted for 41% of all felons convicted of forgery, fraud and embezzlement.[83] Once again, changes in our nation's social fabric have been linked to this phenomenon. For example, the increase in the number of single mothers who must support a household may offer a financial explanation for the increase in female perpetrators. As Haantz points out in her research, the overall percentage of women in the population has not changed much during the last 20 years. However, the number of single mother households jumped from 3 million in 1970 to more than 10 million in 2000. By 2001, women accounted for 47.1% of full-time wage earners in executive, managerial and administrative fields. All of these factors have led to an increase in the opportunity and perceived need among women offenders to carry out such insider activities.

It is also interesting to note that studies of employee theft and embezzlement, especially among women, show similar psychological stressors and "triggers" to that of the male-dominated industrial espionage cases we've studied thus far. For example, employee theft and embezzlement are known to often occur alongside high rates of other deviant or criminal behavior in the workplace. The same stressors or triggers that can lead a person (male or female) to steal proprietary data or conduct industrial espionage can also lead to outright theft and embezzlement in the financial services industry; for example, high levels of workplace stress, dissatisfaction with management, personal financial problems, drug or alcohol habits, and high employee turnover rates stemming either from management-driven re-organizations or outsourcing can lead otherwise honest people to do bad things.

.. -. ... .. -.. . / .--- --- -...

In August 2004, the U.S. Secret Service and the Carnegie Mellon Software Engineering Institute released the results of a year-long study of insider incidents in the banking and finance sector of the economy. It was the first such attempt to focus on a specific industry sector and the means by which malicious insiders in that sector took advantage of their access and knowledge.

The study analyzed 23 incidents that were carried out by 26 insiders throughout the banking and finance industry between 1996 and 2000. The incidents studied took place at a wide variety of businesses, from credit unions to banks, investment firms, credit bureaus, and various other companies whose primary lines of business fall within the banking and financial sector. Of the 23 incidents, 15 involved fraud, four involved theft of intellectual property, and four involved sabotage to IT systems or networks.

Among the most surprising findings of the Secret Service study is the overall lack of technical skill required for these insiders to carry out their crimes. In fact, in 87% of the cases studied the insiders simply used simple and legitimate user commands to carry out their crimes. Only 13% of the cases studied involved insiders who spoofed the identity of other users on the network or conducted other, more sophisticated technical feats to overcome obstacles to gaining control of a system. Likewise, a paltry 9% of the cases involved the use of hacker programs or custom software scripts.

Unlike the vast majority of external hacker attacks, the insiders who took advantage of their access to the banking and financial sector rarely went out of their way to scan systems for technical vulnerabilities that they could use to gain access to portions of the network that may have been off limits to them. But that is not to say that these insiders didn't use the inherent weaknesses in software and hardware products to their advantage. The reality is that in at least 70% of the cases the insider's knowledge of "systemic vulnerabilities" in the applications, processes and procedures in place was critical to their success. In fact, almost half of the cases involved malicious insiders who used their own user accounts to carry out their crimes. This is a clear indication that they used specific knowledge of their employer's technologies, policies and procedures (or lack thereof) to plan and carry out their criminal endeavors. For example:

> "In one case, an insider who worked for a credit card point-of-sale terminal vendor used social engineering to obtain authentication information from the credit card company help staff. The insider posed as a distraught individual (with a fabricated identity) working for a particular, authorized merchant needing help with a malfunctioning terminal. He was then able to credit his own credit card by reprogramming a terminal using the information he had obtained."[84]

In another case, an insider revealed to the Secret Service that he was intimately familiar with the auditing schedule employed by his institution. "The end of the month was hot, the end of the quarter was hotter, and the end of the year was really hot," he told investigators. As a result, he timed his crimes to avoid these periods of likely auditing.

Given the overall lack of technical sophistication involved in many of these incidents it is not at all surprising that a mere 23% of the crimes were carried out by people employed in "technical" positions. And despite the IT profession's "at risk" rating for insider attacks, only 17% of the insider criminals in the banking and finance sector held system administrator privileges.

There are other aspects of the Secret Service study that are worth noting here. For example, the only four cases studied by the Secret Service and Carnegie Mellon that involved sabotage were carried out by employees who were employed in technical positions and had advanced computing skills.

For example, a currency trader who had developed much of the software used by his employer to record, manage, confirm, and audit trades, wrote the software in a way that allowed him to conceal his illegal trades. He even improved the software over time, evolving its capabilities to facilitate different methods of hiding his activities, which included manipulating bank records to make his trading losses look like major gains for the bank in order to keep his job and obtain annual performance bonuses. According to the Secret Service, it was nearly impossible for internal auditors to detect his activities. However, the insider, who consented to be interviewed for the study, told investigators that problems can arise when "the fox is guarding the henhouse." He was referring to the fact that his direct supervisor was not only responsible for ensuring trades by the insider and his colleagues were legal and compliant, but also managed the auditing department. As a result, when other personnel voiced their concerns about the insider's activities, they were told not to rock the boat for fear the valuable, trusted insider would quit.

This lack of imagination on the part of senior management, and the weakness of existing policies and procedures were compounded by several technical security weaknesses that the insider was able to exploit. For example, the employer was guilty of allowing poor password management practices to go unchanged. It was widely known throughout the firm that the default password for each user corresponded to the trader's office number. This enabled the criminal insider to further conceal his activities by using another employee's account on several occasions.

The vast amount of indications and warning data available prior to many of the insider incidents in the banking and finance industry supports the notion that technical enforcement mechanisms are of far greater importance than established policies and procedures. As with every case outlined so far, the policies and procedures established by the banking and finance industry over many years have proven to be ineffectual in the face of determined insiders. For example, in 61% of the cases studied by the Secret Service, co-workers, friends or family members of the accused said they knew something about the insider's plans and intentions. More important, in 35% of the cases, the insider engaged in activities that (as we will see in our study of real-world network activity captured by Reconnex Corp. during their many 48-hour Risk Assessments) clearly pointed to pre-incident planning. Such activities included communicating with an employer's competitors, communicating with co-conspirators and working on and storing malicious software on an employer's network.

It should come as no surprise that the motive behind the vast majority (81%, according to the Secret Service) of insider incidents in the banking and finance sector has always been and continues to be money. More than a quarter of the insiders apprehended for crimes had experienced financial difficulties prior to the incident. But what is more striking is the large percentage of cases (15-25%) that involved a desire for revenge, a need to strike out at what was perceived to be a corrupt corporate culture, and a longing for respect.

Unlike the many espionage cases involving theft of classified or trade secret information, a whopping 42% of the insider crimes committed in the banking and finance sector were committed by women (ages 18-59). This makes the banking and finance industry somewhat unique in terms of what we know about the history of insider activity in other industries. It is also unique from the standpoint of what we know about the opinions of young men versus young women when it comes to overcoming moral and ethical obstacles to malicious activities. Unfortunately, the Secret Service and Carnegie Mellon study offers no insight into what makes women in the banking industry different.

If the Secret Service study is accurate in its findings about how the majority of malicious insiders were discovered, then it is safe to say that the banking and finance sector is in a state of disarray and confusion about how to deal with the insider threat. For example, in at least 35% of the cases the insider's activities were brought to the attention of the institution not by internal security personnel but by a customer. This is the equivalent of a bank teller hitting the panic button the day after the robbery. In fact, security personnel failed to demonstrate a significantly better ability to detect insider abuse than non-security personnel. While one can put a positive spin on that by concluding that non-security personnel must be benefiting from security awareness training, what it really shows is that many security practitioners do not have the appropriate tools to do their jobs.

The financial loss associated with many of these insider crimes is staggering. One out of three cases involved a loss of $500,000 or more. But this is nothing compared to the potential losses that could easily result from the activities that continue to go unnoticed by banks, financial institutions and independent surveys.

The Reconnex Risk Assessment

Banks and financial institutions have many other forms of insider problems that they are not dealing with effectively. In multiple 48-hour live assessments using the Reconnex iGuard system, senior executives watched in dismay as social security numbers, credit card numbers and other privacy-protected financial data were communicated outside of the enterprise in clear text without the security of encryption. In other words, volumes of data that executives never imagined would ever leave the protected confines of their organizations' networks were not only regularly being communicated to known and unknown destinations outside of the enterprise, but often with little or no security protection. Yet every institution that underwent a Reconnex risk assessment said they had an official policy requiring the use of encryption for sensitive data.

In January 2005, a risk assessment at a major financial institution uncovered unencrypted communications of employee 401K contributions, including names, social security numbers and account numbers. And as with many other companies in many other industries, this particular institution appears to have had a major problem with employees downloading and sharing image files and multimedia files. During the 48 hours that the Reconnex technology was deployed on this particular institution's network, 30% of the traffic was identified as images (JPEGs, GIFs, etc…) and 13% was identified as multimedia, such as MP3 music files and MPEG movie files. The presence of large quantities of image files in a business enterprise is often indicative of non-work related activities, such as online shopping and, quite often, pornography.

Management executives responsible for the safe and effective operation of this financial institution had no idea that such sensitive information was leaving their network in clear text format. Likewise, they had no idea that they were facing serious worker productivity issues (i.e. the large number of multimedia files being downloaded in just 48 hours indicates large amounts of enterprise bandwidth being used for non-work-related activities). More important, these executives were unaware of the regulatory, compliance and legal threat they faced stemming from the apparent lack of internal controls and the prevalence of adult content on their corporate network.

Reconnex engineers Joe Godsil and David Cambridge conducted the installation and forensics analysis at this institution and presented the results of the chief financial officer. "We sat down with the CFO and reviewed the report," said Cambridge. "Since Joe had already shown him the spreadsheet with the 401K information, he was not surprised, but did admit that it should not have happened and that they had taken steps to prevent it from happening in the future. Other parts of the report of interest were the multimedia and image files. We see different types of reactions from executives; in this case he played most everything pretty close to the vest with a minimum reaction."

After delivering the report, however, Godsil and Cambridge gave the executive access to the iGuard system so that he could run his own queries on the data. "I am not sure whether it was the report or something he saw running queries, but he called back a couple of days later and said he was buying."

.. -. ... .. -.. . / .--- --- -...

In April 2005, Reconnex installed their system and conducted a 48-hour risk assessment at one of the nation's top 20 financial institutions. This particular institution has thousands of employees around the country and manages more than $80 billion in private assets. But this firm is a legal and regulatory disaster waiting to happen.

Within 48 hours of conducting their live risk assessment, the system logged more than 1.1 million content objects totaling more than 8 gigabytes of data. Among that data was a spreadsheet containing 200 customer names, their account numbers, account balances and tax identification numbers.

Worse still, the spreadsheet was intercepted as it was being transmitted to a personal EarthLink e-mail account. And the story, as outlined in the confidential risk assessment report, only gets worse.

> "We discovered over **4,000** instances of customer Social Security numbers sent in an insecure format. [Ninety] **90** of these Social Security numbers discovered were originally issued to California residents (who may no longer be legal residents of California) but should still be investigated with regard to California's SB 1386 [privacy law]. We believe that by allowing employees to communicate [a] customer's private data to affiliates in an insecure manner, [this financial institution] is needlessly putting itself at considerable risk and not following the Federal Trade Commission's (FTC) guidance on compliance with the Gramm-Leach-Bliley Act."

In stark contrast to the financial firm's publicly stated privacy policy regardng communication between employees and customers, Reconnex technicians discovered that employees of the firm routinely sent customers information in clear text that contained social security numbers, names, addresses, date of birth, driver license numbers, account numbers and account balances. And while the firm in question has made considerable efforts to develop a strong privacy policy and build a secure e-mail system, only 12% of the information monitored was encrypted – a specific recommendation of the Gramm-Leach-Bliley Act. In addition, one e-mail from an employee of the firm to a customer requested the customer to e-mail their name, address and date of birth to open an account – a clear violation of the financial institution's own corporate governance policy, as well as an extreme example of poor security. "We believe that by allowing employees to continue to bypass the secure e-mail system, [the financial firm] is needlessly putting itself at considerable risk," concluded the Reconnex analysts.

Technicians also uncovered a substantial amount of instant messenger (IM) communications that indicated the potential existence of insider trading activity. The Reconnex system found numerous instances of stock recommendations being communicated using AOL IM. "During the 48-hour e-Risk Assessment, we discovered IM with downgrade information on [a major storage networking firm]," the Reconnex analysts wrote in their confidential report to the financial firm.[85] "These IM's took place on the same day that the downgrade was disclosed publicly by [the financial institution]. If this communication took place *prior* to the public release, then this could be a violation of securities laws on insider trading and expose the firm to action from the SEC. This event warrants investigation and allows [the firm] to consider a longer-term strategy for IM monitoring that is in accord with SEC and NASD regulations."

And like most other industries, the finance and banking sector also struggles with a substantial volume of adult content flowing over corporate networks. During the 48-hour risk assessment, the Reconnex system tagged multiple instances of graphic, adult images moving in and out of the financial firm's network. And the security technicians at the firm had invested heavily in security systems designed to filter out adult content. The system also uncovered instances of peer-to-peer file sharing, which needlessly exposed the institution to hacker intrusions that could put its customer data at risk.

"If any of the liability issues outlined above occur, this could create serious damage to the [financial firm's] brand and reputation," wrote Reconnex analysts in their net assessment of the potential damage stemming from the audit findings

.. -. ... .. -.. . / .--- --- -...

There is considerable data to support the conclusion that the internal security threats highlighted above have led to disaster at other, less fortunate institutions. And one of the most significant impacts has been in the area of stock price.

On February 15, 2005, for example, news reports announced a security breach at ChoicePoint, an Alpharetta, Georgia-based company that maintains personal profiles of nearly every U.S. consumer, which it sells to employers, landlords, marketing companies and about 35 U.S. government agencies. As a result of one of the largest identity theft cases in history, the company sent warning letters to 35,000 consumers advising them to check their credit reports for suspicious activity.

By April 14, another major firm was the subject of news stories and an investigation into a security incident involving the loss of customer credit card numbers it had stored on its internal servers. Within two days of the news about the incident at Ralph Lauren, a major clothing designer and retailer, the company lost as much as $2 a share, translating to a more than $200 million loss in value for Ralph Lauren shareholders.

News Story

Indiana man charged with hacking into former employer's systems

He could face 10 years in prison and a $250,000 fine

News Story by Linda Rosencrance

AUGUST 24, 2004 (COMPUTERWORLD) - A Columbus, Ind., man was charged yesterday in federal court with hacking into the systems of his Gloucester, Mass.-based former employer.

Patrick Angle, 34, was charged with one count of intentionally damaging a protected computer belonging to Varian Semiconductor Equipment Associates Inc., according to a statement from the U.S. attorney's office in Massachusetts.

The charge alleges that Angle, who worked for Varian first in Gloucester and then from his home in Indiana, became disgruntled with the company because in September 2003 he was told that his contract would be terminated a month later.

According to the U.S. attorney's office, on Sept. 17, 2003, Angle logged into Varian's server from his home in Indiana and intentionally deleted the source code for the e-commerce software he and others had been developing.

He then covered his tracks by editing and deleting some of the logs of computer activity on the server and by changing the server's root password to make it difficult for other Varian employees to log onto the server and assess and repair the damage, the statement said.

Although Varian was ultimately able to recover the deleted material from backup systems, the recovery effort cost the company $26,455, according to the U.S. attorney's office.

If convicted, Angle faces a maximum sentence of 10 years in prison, to be followed by three years of supervised release, a fine of up to $250,000 and restitution, according to the statement.

Angle's Indiana attorney couldn't be reached for comment.

Chapter 8

Enron in Your Inbox

Only two things are infinite, the universe and human stupidity, and
I'm not sure about the former.
— Albert Einstein

Within a decade of its founding in 1985, Enron Corp. had become the darling of rich investors and powerful politicians. It quickly grew out of its natural gas industry roots to become a mammoth energy trading firm that routinely dabbled in complicated, high-priced contracts that were second in value only to the company's stock. In that short period of time, the company had clawed its way to a ranking of seven on the Fortune 500 list.

In 2000, the company announced it had increased profits by 300% during the previous two years. It was exactly the kind of news that Wall Street had come to expect from the energy giant. But behind the press releases, earnings reports, shareholder briefings and companywide e-mails that touted the firm's long-term vitality and financial stability, unnoticed tremors were causing cracks in the foundation. By March 2001, press reports began to raise serious questions about Enron's accounting, particularly how it was managing its debt.

In August, the firm's president & CEO, Jeffrey Skilling, informed chairman Kenneth Lay that he was resigning. In hindsight, it was the first evidence that the cracks in the Enron foundation had reached the top echelon of the company. Then, vice president Sherron Watkins sent Lay an anonymous letter that warned of a pending crisis stemming from the company's accounting methods. The language she used was fortuitous: If left unchecked, Enron's accounting practices could cause the company to "implode" from the pressure of never-ending "accounting scandals."

So Kenneth Lay did what everybody now knows he was best at doing. He threw up a smoke screen. It was a smoke screen meant both for his employees and his sugar daddies on Wall Street.

In the following e-mail – one of 1.6 million e-mails and calendar entries made public on March 23, 2003 by the Federal Energy Regulatory Commission (FERC) as part of the investigation into Enron, Lay informs the company about Skilling's departure and paints a picture of a company that, despite this minor setback, remained on the road to greatness.

> From: Ken Lay –
> Sent: Tuesday, August 14, 2001 5:01 PM
> To: All Enron Worldwide
>
> Subject: Organizational Announcement (Sent by Enron Announcements/Corp/Enron on behalf of Ken Lay)
>
> It is with regret that I have to announce that Jeff Skilling is leaving Enron. Today, the Board of Directors accepted his resignation as President and CEO of Enron. Jeff is resigning for personal reasons and his decision is voluntary.
>
> I regret his decision, but I accept and understand it. I have worked closely with Jeff for more than 15 years, including 11 here at Enron, and have had few, if any, professional relationships that I value more. I am pleased to say that he has agreed to enter into a consulting arrangement with the company to advise me and the Board of Directors. Now it's time to look forward.
>
> With Jeff leaving, the Board has asked me to resume the responsibilities of President and CEO in addition to my role as Chairman of the Board. I have agreed. I want to assure you that I have never felt better about the prospects for the company. All of you know that our stock price has suffered substantially over the last few months. One of my top priorities will be to restore a significant amount of the stock value we have lost as soon as possible. *Our performance has never been stronger our business model has never been more robust our growth has never been more certain and most importantly, we have never had a better nor deeper pool of talent throughout the company. We have the finest organization in American business today.* [Emphasis added]
>
> Together, we will make Enron the world's leading company. On Thursday at 10:00 a.m. Houston time, we will hold an all employee meeting at the Hyatt. We will broadcast the meeting to our employees around the world where technically available, and I look forward to seeing many of you there.

While Enron's employees were digesting this news and looking positively to the future, Ken Lay was dumping his stock in the company. Then, on Oct. 16, 2001, the firm recorded a $638 million loss. A week later, the Securities and Exchange Commission announced it was investigating the firm. And by Nov. the company had come clean that during the previous four years it had overstated its earnings by $586 million and that it was carrying more than $6 billion in debt – debt that had been hidden from public scrutiny through a series of business partnerships.

It was the beginning of the end for Enron and the nation's introduction to the worst accounting scandal and corporate-fraud criminal undertaking in history.

.. -. ... .. -.. . / .--- --- -...

The murkiness of the Enron corporate culture did more than conceal the company's criminal accounting practices; it also obscured a massive legal liability risk stemming from the inappropriate use of the company's computer network, particularly its e-mail system. In fact, the FERC database of Enron e-mails reveals a company that was at risk of major legal catastrophe long before its accounting scandal ever saw the light of day.

When the FERC first released the Enron e-mail database, it contained more than 1.6 million e-mails, tasks and calendar entries authored by Enron employees at all levels, including the company's high-ranking executives. The initial release of the e-mails included mountains of highly personal information that had been communicated in clear text, including social security numbers, salary information, and bank account records. In fact, one message included an attachment that listed the names, social security numbers and salary information for every employee in the company.

At the behest of many of those employees, however, the personal data was removed by FERC out of fear that the availability of the information could lead to a massive case of identity theft and needless harm to innocent employees of the firm. To accomplish this, FERC conducted searches using obvious terms, such as "kids," "divorce," "social security," and "credit card number." The results were astounding. More than 141,000 e-mails were identified as containing such information and were therefore removed from the database.

That left approximately 91% of the database intact. However, once administrative calendar entries and other mundane task tracking items were removed, the FERC database provided 517,403 e-mail messages for researchers to dig through. And that's exactly what Roger Matus and Sean True, the CEO and chief technologist, respectively, of Audiotrieve LLC, did. In a study titled, "Monsters In Your Inbox: E-mail Liability, Compliance, and Policy Management Risk; A Case Study of the Enron Corporation," Matus and True attempted to find out how many of the Enron e-mails potentially posed a legal or privacy liability risk to the company. What they discovered was not only shocking and scandalous, but reaffirms what the experts at Reconnex Corp. continue to find at hundreds of other enterprises.

Using language analysis technology that they had built into their Inboxer e-mail spam filtering tool, Matus and True found that at least 20% of the e-mails contained non-business related material.[86]

In addition to multiple e-mails detailing personal political views to employees and business partners, one of the first e-mails studied (outlined below) included a detailed discussion of Ken Lay's stress level, including references to his personal health and medications. According to Matus and True, "If such information were released in a timely manner about a public company, it could have an impact on the stock price."

> FROM: "Linda P. Lay"
> TO: Kenneth L. Lay
> DATE = 10/30/2001 TIME : 09:44:07
>
> -----Original Message-----
> From: Phyllis B
> To: Linda Lay
> Subject: RE: Biochemical Research Foundation
> Dear Linda,
> …
> I am concerned about his (Ken's) level of stress, and would highly recommend that he keep up that anxiety control formula, taking two after meals 3x a day. I have stronger things in my arsenal if needed. Also, perhaps when he is here sometime, I could check his blood chemistry for stress factors and optimal brain function.
> Warmest Regards,
> Phyllis

Perhaps the most disturbing aspect of the Enron e-mail database, however, is the sheer volume of inappropriate and sexually explicit e-mails that were circulating around the company. Matus and True discovered that as many as 20,378 e-mails (1 out of every 25) contained pornographic material or image attachments, racially or ethnically offensive content, and dirty jokes. Any one of these e-mails, as verified by the author, could have led to lawsuits arguing the existence of a hostile work environment.

In addition, many of the inappropriate and pornographic images were attached to e-mails that had seemingly innocuous subject lines: "Palm Beach Voters," "Chick from Sask," "The New Democratic seal," "Redneck classifier," "Redneck horseshoes," "You'r Son's First NFL Game," "Lonely?" and "Martha Stewart Holiday Trip." One e-mail, however, did include the subject line "XXX Cartoons."

The author has also independently verified the existence of multiple e-mails that originated from the Enron corporate network environment but were sent using personal Web e-mail accounts. In some of these e-mails, lengthy, graphic descriptions of sexual exploits were outlined using the subject line "The moves..."

Enron's potential e-mail liability nightmare also included inappropriate racial content. "The authors were further shocked by the extent of the problem in some messages," wrote Matus and True. In one message, sent to a large number of recipients, "the text content is about deadbeat fathers, but includes an image of a well-known and reputable civil rights leader superimposed on a young girl's face. The intent is to suggest that this leader is the father of such a child. Messages like this, sent from an official corporate e-mail address, can lead people to believe that the company is not welcoming to minorities."[87]

Some Enron employees also had an insatiable appetite for jokes, particularly jokes about women and women with blonde hair. While many of these jokes could not be classified as pornographic (although there were an ample number of e-mails that were, in fact, pornographic), the sheer volume of e-mails that poked fun at women in the workplace (as verified by the author) could have easily led to legal problems for the company.

Overall, the findings of Matus and True revealed a company that was in great danger of legal and financial ruin many months, if not years, before its accounting irregularities led to criminal charges. The following is a summary of what Matus and True found in Enron's corporate e-mail inbox:

- Nine (9) percent of the messages in the database (141,379 out of 1.6 million) contained personal, confidential information that was so sensitive that it had to be removed from the database.
- Nineteen (19) percent of the messages (98,873 out of 517,403) available for analysis were personal in nature. They could have been confusing or embarrassing because they came from an official e-mail address.
- Four (4) percent of the messages (20,378 out of 517,403) contained inappropriate content such as pornographic content, racially or ethnically offensive language, dirty jokes, or questionable images.

Until recently, the study of Enron's e-mail content was the "gold standard" for understanding the nature of insider liability issues. This has changed, however. When compared with the new data from the Reconnex risk assessments (including the fact that 95% of network traffic today is Web), we can draw the following conclusions: corporate America is awash in inappropriate content (pornography and other legally risky e-mail and Web content), and Enron was neither the first, nor will it be the last, enterprise to be walking the fine line between business success and legal disaster.

News Story

Missing Backup Tapes Spur Encryption at Time Warner

Data security boost follows loss of info on 600,000 employees

News Story by Lucas Mearian

MAY 09, 2005 (COMPUTERWORLD) - Time Warner Inc. last week said it will "quickly" begin encrypting all data saved to backup tapes, after 40 tapes with personal information on about 600,000 current and former employees were lost in transit to a storage facility.

The incident is among the biggest in a string of recent data-security mishaps that have also affected companies such as ChoicePoint Inc., Bank of America Corp. and Reed Elsevier Group PLC's LexisNexis Group unit.

A shipping container that held the 40 data tapes was lost on March 22, Time Warner spokeswoman Kathy McKiernan said. The tapes went missing during a routine shipment to an off-site facility by records management and storage firm Iron Mountain Inc. McKiernan wouldn't provide more details.

However, McKiernan did say Time Warner is trying to convince officials at Boston-based Iron Mountain to change some of their handling procedures. She declined to expand on the status of those discussions.

The $42 billion New York-based media giant also said it has provided the affected employees with resources to monitor their credit reports. The lost tapes didn't include data about Time Warner customers, the company said.

Larry Cockell, Time Warner's chief security officer, added that "we are working closely and aggressively with law enforcement and the outside data-storage firm to get to the bottom of this matter."

Iron Mountain said it has had four incidents of tapes going missing this year. In late April, Ameritrade Holding Corp. in Omaha lost a data tape with the names of 200,000 clients. At the time, the company wouldn't disclose how the tapes were lost, but in an interview last week, Ameritrade CIO Asiff Hirji said that the tape fell off a conveyer belt in a shipping facility.

Assuming the Worst

Hirji, who wouldn't identify the carrier, said that for "whatever reason," the shipper took "a bunch" of tapes out of its original secure box and placed them into another box. Sometime after that, the second box was damaged on the conveyer belt, and four tapes fell out. "We found three," he said. "That other tape, I'm almost 100% sure, is somewhere in that facility—probably in the rubbish bin. Or it has been destroyed in their lost and found. However, we can't take that chance. We have to assume it's lost and has gotten into nefarious hands. I'm not pointing fingers. I'm not deflecting blame. It's our responsibility." Like Time Warner, Ameritrade is taking steps to protect the confidentiality of clients whose names and/or Social Security numbers were on the lost tape. For example, the company has stepped up monitoring to detect whether any identities have been compromised. So far, Hirji said, there has been no evidence of compromised data.

Hirji said Ameritrade is also looking at encrypting data on archive tapes and using shipping boxes that can't be opened so easily.

Melissa Burman, director of corporate communications at Iron Mountain, said her company has stepped up training of employees in the handling of sensitive data on tapes.

"We're doing 5 million pickups and deliveries a year; that's a huge volume. We do have incidents from time to time," she said. "We will look at every opportunity we can to make incremental improvements in our process."

Moreover, Burman said, customers need to encrypt private information on their backup tapes.

Bart Lazar, a privacy and intellectual property lawyer and partner at the law firm Seyfarth Shaw LLP, in Chicago, said that as data-loss incidents pile up, the companies found responsible will likely face pressure to change their data-security standards. Most of the pressure, he noted, won't come from Congress but from insurance companies requiring more stringent safeguards.

Part of the current problem, Lazar said, is that companies don't have proper chain-of-custody requirements or encryption technology in place.

"I've dealt with many of these companies, and if you ask them what happens with their data... they can't chart it," he said. "Or the companies know what to do, and they just haven't committed the resources to do it."

Lazar said data-loss incidents will also likely spur companies to turn to internal data-protection schemes instead of using third-party service providers or external data processors.

Chapter 9

Silicon Valley Shoplifters

"People and companies who steal intellectual property are thieves
just as bank robbers are thieves."
— David W. Shapiro, U.S. Attorney, Northern District of California.

I t's among the most secretive, paranoid and secure organizations on earth.
The iridescent blue glass of the headquarters building shields its inner-
most workings from the hundreds, if not thousands, of spies who would
love an opportunity to roam freely through the halls, office spaces, safes and
laboratories. Here, information is tightly controlled; everything is classified
according to its sensitivity and employees are granted access on a 'need-to-
know' basis. Everything else is encrypted. Security cameras monitor sensitive
work areas. Electronic devices determine who is allowed access to certain
offices and labs, and all access attempts are recorded. Some departments even
have their own security units. Every one of the 85,000 employees is required
to undergo rigorous security training and is then assigned the personal responsibility of enforcing security policies.

From this building some of the world's brightest scientists direct the work
of tens of thousands of people in almost every corner of the globe. Central
control and secrecy, therefore, is paramount. The secrets behind the technologies that have been developed here during the past 35 years require it. In the
wrong hands, they could spell disaster for much of the world's electronic
economy.

Surprisingly, this massive glass complex is not home to the super-secret
National Security Agency (NSA) in Fort Meade, Maryland, or its sister organization, the Defense Intelligence Agency (DIA) at Bolling Air Force Base
in Washington, D.C. In fact, despite its government-like obsession with secrecy and information control this facility isn't home to any of the three-letter
government intelligence organizations. It is the headquarters of the largest
computer chip manufacturer in the world and it is located in Palo Alto, Calif.

Founded in 1968, Intel Corp. develops the silicon engines that power the majority of the world's desktops, servers, laptops, networking devices and communications systems. In addition to its corporate offices, Intel runs 11 fabrication facilities and six test and assembly facilities around the world. In 2003, the company spent $4.4 billion on research and development, supporting the work of more than 7,000 researchers and scientists. It is an organization founded and run upon one thing – brain power. And that, coupled with the revolutionary capabilities of its technologies, makes it one of the biggest targets of international and corporate espionage.

"Alex D.," who asked that his real name be withheld[88], studied artificial intelligence in college and did post-graduate work at Stanford University focusing on microprocessor architecture before joining Intel. His work at Intel touched nearly every modern processor in use today, from the Pentium II through the Itanium processors currently in use. He was heavily involved in the design of Intel's SpeedStep technology and methods to reduce the amount of sub-threshold power leakage that would allow a processor to consume energy without even processing a single instruction. So, Alex understands the sensitivity of Intel's research.

"There was a strict need-to-know policy at Intel," recalls Alex. "You didn't walk into the debug lab or the manufacturing lab unless you had good reason. And when you did your ID card was swiped, you were logged and you were video-taped."

In other words, Intel knows how to keep a secret. For example, in one particular case that occurred in the past few years, a major laptop manufacturer had begun shipping systems that were configured to enter sleep mode between a user's keystrokes when that user was writing a document in Microsoft Word. It was an effort to transparently conserve battery energy. However, a major bug was discovered related to Intel's SpeedStep technology that prevented the systems, in some cases, from coming out of sleep mode. Only six people on the Intel design team knew about the bug and word of the problem never left Intel because it was serious enough, according to Alex, that "it would have been a major stock hit" for the laptop manufacturer.

However, one of the most sensitive areas is that which deals with microcode updates, which are better known as BIOS updates that fix bugs during boot up. This is done through an encrypted interface known as a scan-chain. "To the best of anyone's knowledge, the encryption codes for doing that have never left Intel," said Alex. "It is a secret whose value is on par with the formula for Coke."

To most people, the implications of losing such a secret are unclear. But to Intel and computer security experts, the implications are mind-boggling. In fact, Alex is quick to point out that if a malicious or criminal insider could gain access to those codes and break the security surrounding that microcode updating process they could spark a global security and privacy crisis.

In addition to being able to re-program chips to conduct nefarious operations, such an insider could turn on (activate) IDs and hashes in processors that had those features disabled. These features are often disabled in processors that are sold overseas under export licenses. From the perspective of conducting more overt attacks, Alex has already proven the ability to write code that is capable of disrupting processor operations. While researching power consumption issues at Intel, he and other researchers were able to write code that would cause the AMD K6 processor to reset under special conditions.

"If somebody wanted to cause an Intel processor to re-boot, and had inside knowledge of Intel, they could use any of the spyware holes, any of the stack-overflow bugs and cause major problems [globally]."

But given the company's security restrictions, that somebody would have to be an insider with at least a decade or more time employed at Intel. Still, that doesn't mean it's impossible. "Intel is one insider away from having [its microcode] security system described to the world," said Alex, the former Intel engineer.

The real problem when it comes to malicious microcode updates is that ordinary computer users are not capable of detecting such an attack. And the vast majority of security administrators throughout corporate America are in the same position. That could mean disastrous consequences.

For example, because all modern microprocessors rely on the ability to generate random numbers, a hacker could apply a microcode patch to change the random number function in the processor so that it always returns a known value – making it, in effect, not random at all. This would allow the hacker to attack commercial transactions, secure communications and gain access to any number of secured systems. This should also be a major privacy concern for all citizens of free nations, as such an attack could enable a government agency to circumvent encryption systems to eavesdrop on private communications.

Intel and AMD also face potential brand name damage stemming from unscrupulous vendors and re-sellers of their technology – particularly those with the knowledge and capability to conduct malicious microcode patch updates. Both companies sell microprocessors in speed grades called "bins." And not surprising, processors in higher bins command higher prices on the market, with a relatively small increase in speed (say 15% to 25% increase) commanding a 50% to 100% increase in price.

Again, the average private and corporate user has no way to measure the actual speed of a processor purchased with their computer. They rely, instead, on the results of an instruction – a CPUID – that can display information about the processor to the user. But if a malicious insider obtained information about how to compromise this instruction using a microcode update an unscrupulous vendor could pass off a slower processor as one of its faster, more expensive cousins. It is a scenario that is not at all beyond the realm of possibility. In fact, some vendors in the past are known to have erased the printed speed markings on Intel chips and replaced them with faster markings.

"Compromise of this instruction by the vendor selling the computer would make detection of this type of fraud nearly impossible," said Alex. "Imagine the impact on brand name and the customer confusion that would result if news of such fraud became public."

During my interview with Alex in California, he offered the following worst-case malicious microcode hack scenario, noting that such an attack is possible today only against AMD manufactured processors (at least until a malicious insider manages to leak the Intel information).

> It is April 1, 2007. Using commonly available exploits known to spyware makers everywhere, a malicious hacker constructs a buffer overflow attack causing the victim's computer to download a microcode update patch. If your computer has ever been infected with spyware, this is the exact same process, only this time it is not intended to serve you pop-up advertisements. Instead, the patch replaces all common instructions with an infinite loop – a set of instructions that never finish executing. The hacker's program causes the system to wait seven days and then installs the microcode patch. During this time, the infection spreads silently over the Internet to machines not yet infected.

> At midnight, April 8, 2007, the patches are installed. Suddenly, computers everywhere cease to function and nobody can determine why. The only clues are that the affected systems cannot even boot up from a rescue disk. Discovery of the actual cause would have to come directly from Intel Corp. But the only solution would be wholesale replacement of all affected processors.

> Of course, there aren't enough chips available to meet this type of demand. Meanwhile, more systems are crashing and the Internal Revenue Service has to postpone the April 15 filing deadline for taxes. Business disruption could best be described as total.

In an interview in April 2000, Intel's former director of corporate information security, Marilyn Koch, acknowledged the challenge the company faces from cyber espionage and said it was the threat to corporate secrets that forced the company to take steps that likened it more to a government agency than a chip manufacturer.[89] And Intel is not alone.

Other high-profile technology developers in the U.S. have made serious attempts to lower their risk to insider espionage. Microsoft Corp., for example, physically separates its development community, which holds the keys to the Microsoft technology kingdom, from the firm's sales and support divisions. And like Intel, the company also classifies its data according to sensitivity.

Cisco Systems Inc., the San Jose, Calif.-based global leader of the networking market with 35,000 employees worldwide, has gone as far as to formalize a counterespionage program. The company's Lab Asset Management Program (LAMP) focuses on Cisco's three pillars of protecting proprietary data: education and awareness, physical security standards, and inventory tools for lab assets. But it's only one part of a company-wide campaign, which includes security training for all employees, strict access controls to R&D areas and information, and an automated inventory of ongoing research and product development.

.. -. ... .. -.. / .--- --- -...

On October 9, 1997, Intel announced to the world that the first member of a new, ground-breaking family of 64-bit microprocessors, code-named Merced (named after a river in California), would enter production in 1999. Although highly-anticipated, the news sparked talk of another revolution in the computing world.

Merced was to be produced using Intel's 0.18 micron process technology, which at that time was still under development – another tightly held secret. The processor was being designed to extend the Intel Architecture to new levels of performance, especially for high-end computing environments, such as graphics and scientific applications. Central to that performance enhancement was a three-year joint research endeavor with Hewlett-Packard Co. to develop a new Instruction Set Architecture for 64-bit computing. Although the companies remained tight-lipped about the processor's eventual speed and the inner workings of its fabrication, the word throughout Silicon Valley was that Merced would match, if not exceed, the speed of Digital Equipment Corp.'s Alpha chip – speeds of 1 gigahertz and higher.

Meanwhile, the software industry was busy lining up behind the new processor capability. The Unix development community was already there. But others, like Microsoft, were readying their own products, such as a 64-bit Windows operating system for Merced. Likewise, various workstation manufacturers, even Silicon Graphics, were planning to announce their support for the new chip on the block.

But inside Intel something else was happening.

Say Lye Ow was a 31-year-old Malaysian citizen living in Sunnyvale, Calif., and working as an engineer at Intel. One of the primary projects he worked on was the new 64-bit Merced processor, now known as the Itanium. His access provided him with detailed information on the future road map of Intel's new line of processors. It was clear to Ow that such information could come in handy in the future. Perhaps it could make him some money? Or, more important, perhaps such knowledge could make him a shining star, indispensable, in his next job? So on July 24, 1998, Ow decided to copy secret design documents related to the Itanium. He would later take them with him and store them on his work computer at his new employer – chief Intel rival Sun Microsystems.

It was at Sun where the secret Intel documents were discovered, but federal law enforcement officials found no evidence that any of Intel's intellectual property had been passed to Sun or any other competitor. However, while Sun cooperated fully with the investigation and is not mentioned in the indictment of Ow, Intel eventually dropped mention of Sun in its marketing material as a key supporter of the Itanium processor, alleging that the company was not serious in its support.

In a plea agreement filed on Sept. 14, 2001 in a U.S. District Court in San Jose, Ow acknowledged in writing that he knowingly copied the material with the intent to use it for financial gain.

> I copied without authorization computer files relating to the design and testing of the Merced microprocessor (now known as the Itanium microprocessor). I knew at the time that it was a trade secret belonging to Intel Corp. I copied that trade secret with the intent to convert it to my own economic benefit by using it at my new employment.[90]

On Dec. 11, 2001, U.S. District Judge Jeremy Fogel sentenced Ow to two years in prison.

"People and companies who steal intellectual property are thieves just as bank robbers are thieves," said U.S. Attorney David Shapiro. "In this case, the Itanium microprocessor is an extremely valuable product that took Intel and HP years to develop. These cases should send the message throughout Silicon Valley and the Northern District that the U.S. Attorney's Office takes seriously the theft of intellectual property and will prosecute these cases to the full extent of the law."

.. -. ... .. -.. . / .--- --- -...

Microsoft has also taken great strides to protect its intellectual property, particularly the source code for its Windows operating system – which it refers to as the "crown jewels" of the company. Source code never leaves the Microsoft corporate campus and is only shared with a limited number of developers outside of the company, including some government agencies, all of which are required to sign legal non-disclosure agreements. And those agreements do more than forbid the developers from sharing the code; they require all who are granted access to provide a certain level of security to prevent criminal or inadvertent disclosure of Microsoft's secrets. Yet, like Intel, Microsoft has experienced the pain and anguish of losing closely guarded secrets.

In early Feb. 2004, FBI special agent Frank Manzi read several news reports about a security breach at the software giant that led to the loss of the bare source code that powered the Windows NT 4.0 and Windows 2000 operating systems. By Feb. 12, Microsoft had learned that large chunks of the source code for the two operating systems (each individual copy of which was worth several hundred dollars on the retail market and used primarily by business environments) had indeed been stolen and were now showing up on the public Internet. Immediately, Manzi was briefed on the case.

With the help of private investigators hired by Microsoft to look into the breach, Manzi's investigation led him to William P. Genovese, a 27-year-old living in Meriden, Conn. Genovese, who had a prior record of computer hacking, would eventually be charged in Manhattan U.S. District Court with unlawfully distributing a trade secret.

A Microsoft lawyer told *The New York Times* the arrest was "significant," given the value of the intellectual property. "It is our secret recipe, our secret formula like the Coke formula," said Microsoft associate general counsel Tom Rubin. Genovese, who went by the online nickname "illwill," was selling the Windows code on a Web site for as little as $20.

In an interesting twist, however, analysis of the stolen code – estimated to be about 660 megabytes in size, or about 15% of the total size of the Windows source code base – revealed that it was likely stolen from a Microsoft partner firm, Mainsoft Corp. The San Jose, Calif.-based company was one of two firms specializing in Unix-to-Windows interoperability that were granted access to the code. Mainsoft was not, however, a member of Microsoft's Shared Source Initiative, which grants code access to 300 developer partners and government agencies for review.

One particular reference to Mainsoft was noted in a file named "download.cpp." The file contained a statement that the API (Application Program Interface) had not yet been implemented by Mainsoft and that it required an extra check on Unix.

But for some analysts that wasn't proof enough that the leak originated within Mainsoft. In fact, some analysts who reviewed the leaked code said it appeared to have been manipulated before being made available online. Some parts of the code, which included portions of the kernel, appeared to be very high quality, while other portions appeared to be sloppy.

Microsoft, on the other hand, was steadfast in its contention that no security breach had occurred in either its internal or external security controls.

But Genovese, who maintained he was guilty of nothing more than receiving and viewing the stolen code, was not convinced that Microsoft had not suffered a breach. In an interview given on Nov. 11, 2004 to former hacker-turned-journalist Kevin Poulsen, Genovese claimed the real thief remained at large.

"They're using me as an example, to show if you do something like this, they're going to [work] you over," Genovese told Poulsen. "Why go after me? Why not go after the guy who took the code? Why not go after the guy who released it on the net?"[91]

At the time of this writing, the charges against Genovese were merely accusations and a court decision had not yet been reached in the case.

.. -. ... .. -.. . / .--- --- -...

The case against Igor Serebryany, however, has already been decided. The 19-year-old University of Chicago student was convicted in 2003 of stealing trade secrets belonging to DirecTV.

The digital satellite television provider reaches millions of Americans around the country. Those familiar with the service know that it takes more than an account with DirecTV, a satellite dish and a satellite signal receiver; it also requires a smart card that is inserted in a slot in the back of the receiver that authorizes receipt of the digital signal. One of those cards was the DirecTV Period 4 access card, and it cost the company $25 million to develop. DirecTV worked for years with its security partners to develop the card because all three previous versions had been cracked by hackers, enabling them to decode the encrypted signals and circumvent DirecTV programming controls.

DirecTV has spent millions of dollars trying to combat unauthorized access to its programming signals, including preventing legitimate users from exceeding their authorized programming packages. The company has employed a wide variety of methods to accomplish this, including electronic countermeasures to jam counterfeited or illegally modified smart cards. However, the company has been up against an organized "pirate community" that is engaged in an aggressive program to continually develop ways to beat DirecTV's countermeasures and feed a black market in illegal access cards.

In 1997, DirecTV took its first step to address the problem by contracting with a company called NDS Americas Inc. to develop a replacement access card for the company's first generation of cards. The so-called Period 2 card was then developed and distributed to all DirecTV subscribers. But the hacker community quickly developed a way around the card's security.

By Feb. 1999, DirecTV incurred great expense to develop a third generation of security-enabled access cards – the Period 3 card. The first hacked versions of the Period 3 card were announced by the pirate underground in Nov. 2000.

The Period 4 card, or the Fourth Generation smart card, was the result of two years of research and development by DirecTV and its security partner

NDS. In addition to the extreme R&D cost, the card is said to include proprietary DirecTV technologies that had until that time never been used in a smart card application.

At the time, Serebryany was living in the Los Feliz area of Los Angeles, Calif., and was working for a copying service that had been hired by Jones Day Reavis & Pogue, the Los Angeles-based law firm representing DirecTV in a civil litigation case against one of its security vendors.

In Sept. 2002, DirecTV and Jones Day began preparing for their case. Part of that preparation involved sharing secret documents pertaining to the Period 4 access card with lawyers from the firm. Some of the data shared with the law firm was so sensitive that DirecTV had stored it in a secure facility and in encrypted format.

But on October 10, executives at Jones Day telephoned the local U.S. attorney's office and the FBI about a theft of trade secrets belonging to DirecTV and NDS. Responding to the call were Assistant U.S. Attorney James W. Spertus, FBI special agent Christopher Beausang, and FBI special agent Tracy Marquis Kierce. When they arrived at Jones Day, they met with Larry Rissler, the vice president of Signal Integrity at DirecTV, Joshua I. Halpern, director of Threat Management Services for the Internet Crimes Group, Inc., and attorneys from the law firm. The story told that day and the ensuing investigation revealed that DirecTV's trade secrets had been compromised once again and the evidence was pointing to somebody on the inside.

.. -. ... .. -.. . / .--- --- -...

The story begins in August 2002, when DirecTV and its legal counsel, Jones Day, began preparing the paperwork to support a civil case against NDS for breach of contract. Executives from DirecTV delivered to Jones Day lawyers in Los Angles 27 boxes of documents, many of which had until that time only existed in secure electronic form.

Jones Day immediately set-up a case room to store the boxes of documents belonging to DirecTV. Access to the room was strictly controlled and limited to the law firm's legal assistants and lawyers who were working on the case and had a need to know what information was contained in the documents. It was in this room that legal assistants spent much of their time compiling lists of documents that were deemed critical to the case against NDS. As a result, many of these documents had to be copied as soon as possible so that they could be placed in case binders.

Jones Day maintained an imaging center on the premises of its corporate headquarters. On-site photocopying was deemed the best way to ensure the documents didn't fall into the wrong hands. So, the boxes that had been marked for copying were sent from the case room to the imaging center, which was operated by a firm called Uniscribe.

Once again, access to the documents was limited to only a select few employees at Uniscribe. Each employee – Yelena Tsvetkova, Peker L. Mikhaie (aka Michael Peker) and Abraham Filoteo – were required to read and adhere to a written policy governing control and access to the documents and the confidentiality requirements governing their content.

The process of copying paper documents sounds simple enough. But at Jones Day, that process was anything but simple. There were six computers that were used to scan the documents into electronic format. The scan created a TIF image file. After scanning, numbering codes and confidentiality statements were appended to the image files. The image files were then scanned using optical character reader (OCR) technology to create an additional text file. At that point, the TIF images and the OCR files were written to CDROMs that were either stored in the imaging center or provided to Jones Day attorneys. Seems like the end of the process, right? Wrong.

Surprisingly, an additional hard copy of each document, called a "blowback," was then created. Those too were either stored temporarily in the imaging center or provided to attorneys. Finally, the hard copy documents would be scanned and stored in digital form on storage media connected to the computers in the imaging center. From an information security and control standpoint, this was a disaster waiting to happen.

On Sept. 6, DirecTV and Jones Day presented their case to a federal court. Because the case would involve discussions of ongoing research and development – the bulk of which was based on trade secrets belonging to DirecTV – the complaint and related documents were kept under seal to ensure that the pirate and hacking communities did not gain access to secret data pertaining to the Period 4 access card.

But the case was far from over and there were more documents that needed to be copied. On Sept. 13, Jones Day requested Uniscribe to begin working overtime to get all of the documents copied. As many as 22 of the 27 boxes that had been earmarked for copying were now delivered to the imaging center for photocopying. Uniscribe agreed to do whatever was necessary to get the job done. And it was at that time that a fourth person volunteered his services to the copying team that had been assigned to the DirecTV case. His name was Igor Serebryany.

.. -. ... .. -.. . / .--- --- -...

At 6:45 PM on Sept. 16, 2002, a user who went by the nickname Igor32 conducted a Google search using one of the six computers in the Jones Day imaging center. The computer was connected to the public Internet to provide employees with e-mail connectivity. The user entered his search term: Vcipher. In seconds, references to the popular pirate site appeared on the screen. Among the search results was another interesting site: DSS-Hackers.com.

Igor then located MAXXIMUS, the Web site administrator of DSS-Hackers. He drafted an e-mail to MAXXIMUS in which he stated that he had internal documents and secret information that belonged to DirecTV and NDS. Igor emphasized that he would only have access to the documents for a short time and he wanted desperately to get them posted on the Internet. Time was running out, Igor said, especially since he had to first convert the documents into Adobe Acrobat format before e-mailing them.

MAXXIMUS pondered the identity and motive of his new friend. Perhaps he was a disgruntled former employee of one of the companies? Perhaps he was a hacker who got lucky or an insider looking to make some money? It didn't matter. But a sample would be nice.

Igor sent MAXXIMUS a few documents through Yahoo! Messenger. MAXXIMUS realized immediately that his new friend was for real. But Igor had too many documents for MAXXIMUS to upload to his Hong Kong-based Web server. So he forwarded the documents on Igor's behalf to Pirates-Den.com, an online forum dedicated to sharing information about how to circumvent the security controls of DirecTV's satellite signals. He then told Igor that he knew somebody who could help him find a place to upload the rest of the documents. MAXXIMUS then cut off all communications with Igor and destroyed the few documents he had received. It was a wise move.

The moderator of MAXXIMUS' Web site said he had a friend in Canada who maintained a server that would allow Igor to use FTP (File Transfer Protocol) to upload as many documents as he wanted. Igor then made several CDs containing the DirecTV and NDS documents using one of the computers in the Jones Day imaging center. He placed the CDs in a CD holder labeled "The Doors LA Woman" so that they would appear to be music files. Igor took the CDs home and used his parents' high-speed Digital Subscriber Line (DSL) Internet connection to upload the files.

Within days, more than 800 megabytes worth of trade secrets pertaining to the Period 4 access card – the only access card that criminals had not yet figured out how to crack – appeared on PiratesDen.com. The documents that were posted on the site included highly secret internal design schematics and internal correspondence between DirecTV engineers and NDS security experts that discussed the architecture of the cards and its security features. It was a worst case scenario. Everything that DirecTV and Jones Day had been doing to protect the intellectual property secrets involved in the case was for naught.

.. -. ... .. -.. . / .--- --- -...

On October 10, Jones Day executives began the process of sealing off the imaging center and hired a computer forensics expert to begin investigating and collecting evidence that might prove who was responsible for the breach.

Meanwhile, NDS was quick to state that they had nothing to do with the loss of the data and that the source of the leak was likely inside DirecTV.

While it was certainly possible that somebody inside DirecTV was responsible for sending the documents to the pirate Web site, the FBI considered it unlikely. DirecTV employed extraordinary security measures, relying on the practices of its parent company Hughes Electronics Corp. – a trusted military contractor. Among the measures taken to protect its most sensitive information is a requirement for all employees to sign a confidentiality agreement that remains in force even after their employment. In addition, color-coded badges tell security personnel whether a person is an employee, a contractor or a visitor and restrict where they can go within the facility. Visitors must inform a cadre of professional security officers manning the facility's entrance checkpoints if they are carrying a computer and all bags are subject to search upon leaving.

A separate building houses the DirecTV engineering spaces, is guarded by a separate security force and is served by a security-controlled elevator system. And even within this separately guarded and secured building, some engineers are granted conditional access to highly sensitive programs, such as the smart card development program. Those who are granted access to such programs must not only be able to get into the engineering building and onto the engineering floor, bust must also have access to a special room that is secured with cipher locks, the combinations of which are known only to a handful of DirecTV employees. Wall-mounted security cameras monitor this area 24 hours per day, seven days per week.

From an information and communications security perspective, DirecTV employs a strict, military-like need-to-know policy for information access control. Likewise, all third party contractors, such as chip manufacturers, are assigned code names and are only referred to by those code names in all communications and correspondence within DirecTV and with outside entities. In addition to segregation of all computer networks in the engineering spaces and restriction of all external connections to those networks, all correspondence referring to the company's intellectual property is required to be printed on color-coded paper that offers quick identification of the sensitive information. However, no information related to the super-secret Period 4 access card ever existed in hard copy format. That is, not until the lawsuit against NDS.

By Nov. 15, the investigation was coming together. The forensics expert hired by Jones Day had determined that secret information pertaining to DirecTV had indeed left the facility. Special agents Kierce and Beausang then drove to the Jones Day imaging center and began collecting evidence. They confiscated hand-written work schedules that showed Igor Serebryany had worked during the times of the alleged uploading of the documents to the pirate Web sites. In addition, a printout from a surveillance camera showed Serebryany entering the facility at 10:39 a.m. on the morning of Sept. 22.

The FBI agents interviewed Serebryany on Dec. 17 at the bureau's Los Angeles Field Office. They explained to him why he was being questioned and that they were trying to determine the facts surrounding the leak of the DirecTV secrets. Serebryany acknowledged creating two compact discs containing TIF image files of DirecTV documents and searching for the pirate Web sites using a computer at the Jones Day imaging center where he worked. He also told the agents that he converted the files on the disc to Adobe PDF format using his parents' computer at his home and outlined his attempts to transmit the files to the hacking and pirate community.

The FBI had their man. Despite the extraordinary security measures undertaken by DirecTV to control access within the confines of their protected buildings, Igor Serebryany managed to become a "trusted insider" without ever setting foot in a DirecTV office.

Authorities arrested Serebryany at his home in Los Angeles on Jan. 2, 2003. He pled guilty to theft of trade secrets on April 18 of that year. U.S. District Judge Lourdes G. Baird sentenced him on Sept. 8 to home detention for six months and five years probation, and ordered him to pay $146,085 in damages.

.. -. ... .. -.. . / .--- --- -...

The Reconnex Risk Assessments

In January 2005, technicians from Reconnex Corp. installed the company's monitoring device on the network of one of the largest technology companies in the nation. During the 48-hour risk assessment, the system captured 414 individual posts to stock message boards, indicating a major potential problem with employees leaking confidential company data and plans as a means to boost the price of the stock or, worse, undermine the company's financial performance.

In addition, multimedia files comprised 28% of the network traffic analyzed in those 48 hours. Large numbers of multimedia files in this particular business environment is an indication of employee productivity problems as well as potential legal liability problems stemming from the downloading of pornographic material. The following chart depicts the actual number and types of files discovered traversing the network:

Shockwave	128,970
RealMedia	2,275
ASF (Advanced Streaming audio/video)	1,880
MPEG	1,157
MP3	615
MIDI	318

MPlayer	73
AVI	65

Technicians also noted 46,000 instances of peer-to-peer file sharing taking place in connection with popular file-sharing Internet sites, such as eDonkey, Gnutella and Bit Torrent. But the potential losses of intellectual property and legal dangers from the exposure of privacy-protected data get much worse.

For example, one employee at this major technology firm was apparently managing applications for a baseball coaching position. During the risk assessment period, an unencrypted spreadsheet was noted leaving the network that included personal information on the candidates, including names, phone numbers, addresses and social security numbers.

More important, the Reconnex system intercepted a Powerpoint slide presentation that was clearly marked Company Proprietary and Confidential. Upon further investigation, technicians and company officials discovered that it contained sensitive information about the features, status and architecture of one of the company's main products. That document had been sent out unencrypted as a Yahoo mail attachment to an unknown Hotmail account. In another instance, a proprietary technical design document was sent out of the company by a current employee using Web mail. In the body of the e-mail message, the employee indicated that he was interested in starting his own company in the same industry that his current employer is in.

At least 50 current employees of this particularly technology company were actively searching for a new job at the time of the risk assessment. During the 48 hours that the Reconnex system was operating on the network, more than 50 resumes were identified leaving the network, indicating a significantly higher risk of malicious insider activity.

The amount of Web mail traffic that left the corporate network carrying attachments was of great concern to the corporate executives that were privy to the risk assessment results. For example, the system noted 810 instances of Webmail, including 70 JPEG attachments, 60 Word documents (likely resumes), 10 Excel spreadsheets, 3 Powerpoint and 14 zipped files. This was in addition to 670 instances of proprietary source code – code that is in wide use throughout the public Internet today – that was noted traveling across the company's network unencrypted.

In a perfect example of how even the most sophisticated technology companies have not yet come to grips with the loss of the security perimeter, Reconnex technicians also reported that an unknown user downloaded a training course administration guide to a Web site in Singapore. The guide included detailed course outlines and snippets of intellectual property.

This was a lot for the executives of this company to wrap their minds around. They were, after all, executives of a company noted for its thought leadership in security. But to really get a feel for how much intellectual property was leaking from within their enterprise, the executives designed custom rule sets and asked the Reconnex technicians to input the rules into the system. The custom rules were designed to specifically look for communications between trusted employees and outside competitors. The results were astounding. One of the first documents captured by the system was a planning document that outlined the "strengths, weaknesses, opportunities and threats" of the company's business plan vis-à-vis two of its direct competitors. The company executives had seen enough.

In April 2005, the Reconnex technical team conducted another 48-hour risk assessment at a major high-tech firm. The executives got a good look at what their employees were doing during work hours and the potential legal problems this could cause. The Reconnex system captured more than 75,590 image files that were being transmitted on the company's network, the vast majority of which contained hard-core pornographic content. In addition to the images, 42 chat sessions were logged (33 AOL and 9 Yahoo) including several of an adult nature describing where to get free xxx pictures and videos.

Unfortunately for this company, pornography wasn't their only problem. The system also identified unencrypted spreadsheets leaving the network that contained sensitive financial data. The spreadsheets included fixed asset listings as well as the custodian division name for the assets and expense account numbers. In addition, the system found multiple instances of engineering documents and diagrams leaving the network, as well as 313 instances of source code.

A risk assessment conducted in mid-April 2005, revealed more than a dozen corporate e-mails containing unencrypted social security numbers that were delivered to unknown e-mail addresses on the Internet. One of the e-mails bore the subject line "Stock Information." Another e-mail was tagged "Important" because the sender had discovered errors in his W-2 tax withholding form.

Once again, this particular high-tech company was no different than most other companies when it came to inappropriate content. More than 91,000 image files were noted moving across the network, including many that contained pornographic or inappropriate adult content.

The 48-hour risk assessment at this high-tech firm also discovered more than 220 instances of source code being communicated either within the company or with external entities in unencrypted format. One e-mail attachment detailed the debugging of a network driver commonly in use throughout the Internet.

But the most interesting results stemmed from custom rules that were created by executives from this high-tech firm. The rules were designed to search for items like pricing lists and code words for new technology development initiatives. Company executives uncovered at least three instances of pricing data being posted to the Internet. In addition, the executives searched for a four-letter code word and found 10 Internet postings that referred to the code word.

News Story

Breach of Credit Data May Have Broad Scope

HSBC warns 180k of possible ID thefts; other banks also aware of security gaffe

News Story by Jaikumar Vijayan

APRIL 18, 2005 (COMPUTERWORLD) - An IT security problem involving a U.S. retailer's point-of-sale system (POS) is prompting HSBC Holdings PLC to warn 180,000 of its credit card holders about potential identity theft. And the breach could cause other companies that issue credit cards to take similar actions.

MasterCard International Inc. and Visa U.S.A. Inc. both confirmed last week that they were notified of the systems breach, the latest in a string of security incidents that have come to light since late February. MasterCard and Visa said that in turn, they have informed unspecified numbers of banks and credit card companies about the possibility that data was compromised.

Discover Financial Services Inc. said some of its card holders have also been affected. And American Express Co. said it's aware of the incident but has yet to see "any out-of-pattern activity" with its cards.

In a statement sent via e-mail, Polo Ralph Lauren Corp. confirmed that its POS system stored credit card data instead of purging it immediately after transactions were completed. The statement also noted that the New York-based retailer has been working with law enforcement officials and credit card companies since last fall to determine the origin and extent of the data compromise.

Polo Ralph Lauren said that after learning about the retained information, it "took immediate steps to purge this data and cure the problem." The retailer said it's confident that its credit card system is secure and that customer data is properly protected. It declined to comment further.

Reviewing Strategies

Incidents such as this one are forcing many security managers to review their strategies for protecting data, said Howard Schmidt, chief information security officer at eBay Inc. and a former White House cybersecurity adviser.

"I know a number of CSOs who are getting calls from their executive ranks wanting to know if the same things could happen to them," Schmidt said.

What's needed is a multifaceted plan that addresses various threats, said David Wallace, director of global systems security at Pilgrim's Pride Corp. in Pittsburg, Texas. The recent compromises have been executed through different methods, including social engineering, hardware theft and hacking, he noted. Wallace also pointed to the potential for insider abuse of system-access privileges.

Thomas Nicholson, a spokesman for Prospect Heights, Ill.-based HSBC North America Holdings Inc., said the POS problem affected all credit card transactions conducted at Polo Ralph Lauren between June 2002 and last December. "It's a POS issue," he said. "We just happened to be the first bank to notify customers of the risk."

According to Nicholson, MasterCard informed HSBC of the problem in February and identified customers who may have been affected. HSBC North America, a division of London-based HSBC Holdings, last Monday started asking holders of its General Motors-branded MasterCard who were on the list to replace their cards.

Discover Financial Services Inc. and American Express Co. didn't return calls seeking comment on the problem at Polo Ralph Lauren.

Chapter 10

The Underground

Manufacturing, Retail & Transportation

"Strong intellectual property rights protections and enforcement at home and abroad are critical for the success of America's innovative economy."
– Acting U.S. Trade Representative, Peter Allgeier. April 29, 2005

The continued loss of intellectual property in the U.S. manufacturing, retail and transportation industries has global implications. Not the least of those ramifications is the unfair trade balance that is perpetuated by countries that either have no laws against such theft or fail to enforce the laws properly. While the various individual cases of insider theft and sabotage in the manufacturing industry are certainly significant, it is the global ripple effect of these losses (losses that often lead to foreign interception and counterfeit of innovations made by U.S. companies) that has many people asking a very important question: Is anything really Made In America anymore?

On April 29, 2005, the Office of the U.S. Trade Representative released its annual "Special 301" report on the adequacy and effectiveness of intellectual property rights protection around the world. While the report praised some countries for their efforts, it also found that poor intellectual property protection regimes continue to be a serious problem for the U.S. economy.

Specifically, the report presents a special Out-of-Cycle Review of China's intellectual property regime, and concludes that infringement levels remain unacceptably high throughout China. China was first designated a Priority Foreign Country in 1994 under Section 306 (monitoring) of the Trade Act of 1974. In fact, China's inability or unwillingness to clamp down on intellectual property theft resulted in the Bush administration elevating China to the Priority Watch List for failure to effectively protect intellectual property rights and to meet its commitment to significantly reduce infringement levels. The rate of intellectual property theft and infringement in China is estimated to be at 90% or higher for "virtually every form of intellectual property."

"China must take action to address rampant piracy and counterfeiting, including increasing the number of criminal [intellectual property theft] cases and further opening its market to legitimate copyright and other goods," said Acting U.S. Trade Representative, Peter Allgeier, in a press statement.

Likewise, in 2004 the value of Chinese counterfeits coming into the United States increased 47% from $94 million to $134 million. These seizures accounted for 67% of all U.S. Customs' intellectual property seizures that year. And these counterfeit products threaten public health and safety in the U.S., according to the U.S. Trade Representative report. "Batteries, pharmaceuticals, auto parts, industrial equipment and many other counterfeit products from China come to our shores."

Russia was also named in the report and remains on the U.S. Priority Watch List. "In particular, we remain concerned about high levels of piracy of optical media (CDs and DVDs) and a growing problem with Internet piracy of copyrighted works," the report states.

As of this writing, the U.S. has placed 14 trading partners on the Priority Watch List. These countries are: Argentina, Brazil, China, Egypt, India, Indonesia, Israel, Kuwait, Lebanon, Pakistan, the Philippines, Russia, Turkey, and Venezuela.

.. -. ... .. -.. . / .--- --- -...

Although the intellectual property of U.S. manufacturing and retail companies is not necessarily being protected overseas, there is also much room for improvement here at home. The very companies that are losing a competitive edge to foreign entities that steal and copy their intellectual property have done a less than stellar job of ensuring their own people adequately protect corporate trade secrets.

Starting on July 26, 2002 and ending on August 5, 2002, John Morris placed a series of telephone calls to executives at W.L. Gore & Associates, a global manufacturing company with $1.3 billion in sales from the use of its proprietary technology in electronic signal transmission systems, fabric laminates, medical implants, membrane filtration systems, sealant, and fibers technologies. The first call was simple and to the point. Morris had something to sell; something that would not only directly benefit W.L. Gore's business, but would take them years to develop on their own.

Morris offered the W.L. Gore executives the proprietary pricing information belonging to Brookwood Companies, Inc., a textile manufacturing company based in Manhattan. Brookwood was a direct competitor of W.L. Gore and Morris' employer at the time. He said he would accept $100,000 for the data.

Shortly after receiving Morris' first telephone call and the offer for the pricing information, executives from W.L. Gore contacted federal law enforcement officials and informed them of Morris' actions. Because of the wide array of military-related technologies that W.L. Gore manufactured, the case was investigated by agents from the Defense Criminal Investigative Service.

The agents quickly set up a sting operation. During the next several calls placed to W.L. Gore, Morris was under the impression that he was dealing with a senior W.L. Gore executive. He was actually talking to a Defense CIS agent. The agent agreed to meet Morris on August 5 to pay him his fee and take possession of the proprietary pricing data. The meeting went down at a rest stop on the New Jersey Turnpike, where Morris was easily taken into custody.

On October 17, 2002, John Morris entered a plea of guilty to attempting to steal trade secrets belonging to Brookwood Companies.

Seven months later, on May 23, 2003, William Garrison, a 57-year-old Grand Island, New York resident pled guilty in a U.S. District Court to downloading and attempting to steal proprietary engineering drawings and data belonging to his soon-to-be former employer. According to court documents, Garrison was a 16-year veteran employee of Wendt Corp., a manufacturer of metal shredding equipment based in Tonawanda, New York. A former service technician for the firm, Garrison had access to engineering drawings and trade secret data that the company had developed over a period of decades.

At his plea hearing, Garrison told prosecutors that in April 2002 he decided to leave Wendt Corp. for a similar position outside of the Western New York region. But before he left, Garrison downloaded thousands of engineering files belonging to the company.

Not even the venerable Nestle Company, the world's largest food and beverage company with 247,000 employees worldwide and factories in nearly every country in the world, could escape the poisonous reach of malicious insiders. The case, which involved Nestle's U.S. business, was the first computer crime case brought to court in the Western District of Missouri. The year was 2002.

On Dec. 19 of that year, a grand jury returned an indictment against Richard Gerhardt, a temporary information systems consultant who had been working at the Friskies Petcare plant in St. Joseph. Friskies is one of 15 different pet care product lines manufactured by Nestle U.S. According to the indictment against Gerhardt, between August 12, 2001 and June 10, 2002, he deliberately gained access to the Nestle network computer system without authorization and in excess of his authorized access. Gerhardt allegedly downloaded approximately 5,000 user account passwords from Nestle's system, costing the firm thousands of dollars to conduct a damage assessment and verify the security of its network. Executives were concerned particularly about the integrity of the Nestle global network, which links all of the company's subsidiaries through the corporate headquarters in Vevey, Switzerland.

Prosecutors alleged that Gerhardt used a password-cracking tool named "L0phtCrack" to break the passwords of the various user accounts on the Nestle network. He also allegedly created a database of the user names and passwords, and stored them in a hidden file on the Nestle server, as well as on a laptop issued to him by the company to do his work. In addition to his theft of passwords, prosecutors also said that forensic evidence existed that showed Gerhardt logged into the Nestle network from a remote location and created a new, unauthorized system administrator account. System administrator accounts are very powerful accounts and often provide the user with "root" access to a computer's file system and resources. Using his access to the system, he loaded a program called "pwddump.exe" (password dump) on the Nestle network. The program then communicated with all of the other computers operating on the network at a preset time each day to collect active user accounts and passwords.

Gerhardt pled guilty on March 13, 2002. Under the terms of his plea agreement, the judge ordered him to pay Nestle U.S. the sum of $10,000 – the revised figure of estimated losses that his actions cost the company. He did not do any jail time.

.. -. ... .. -.. . / .--- --- -...

"Dr. Crime" was a hacker before being a hacker was cool. At least that's what he wrote on a Web page that was later found by the FBI during the investigation into his attempt to destroy the electronic infrastructure of his former employer.

His real name was John Michael Sullivan and he was hired on Sept. 23, 1996 by Charlotte, N.C.-based Lance Inc. to help develop a specialized computer system that was to be used by the snack food company's sales force to track sales, inventory and delivery information. But by May 8, 1998, he had been demoted for what company officials described as poor performance. He resigned on May 22.

But before he walked out of the office for the last time on June 2 Sullivan left a present for his former employer.[92] And he didn't leave it at the front desk or on the desk in his cubicle where somebody could easily find it. Like the hacker he proclaimed to be, he left it buried in the Visual Basic code that powered the handheld computers used by the Lance sales and management force. To be specific, he left it hidden in a code module named "printdoc.bas."

"The Lance program contains computer instructions whose only purpose is to disrupt the operation of other parts of the program," said Dr. John F. Repede, the government's expert witness in the case against Sullivan. "This is often referred to as a 'logic bomb' in the computer industry. In addition, the logic bomb contains additional instructions which delay the damage until a certain date and time. This type of logic bomb is often referred to as a 'time bomb'."[93]

Although Sullivan's hacker tradecraft was certainly not unusually sophisticated, it was good enough to wreak havoc on unsuspecting average employees. This is how Sullivan's time bomb worked.

When a route salesman printed a report, the report writing part of the system (printdoc.bas) would check the current time and date. If the current time and date was before 12:00 noon on Sept. 23, 1998, the report writer would carry out its normal functions. But if the current time and date was after 12:00 noon on Sept. 23, the report writer would execute additional instructions that would destroy the part of the program (rasapi.exe) used for communicating with Lance headquarters. And that would, in effect, cut-off the company's sales force from the enterprise and bring the entire operation to a halt.

Repede's testimony also supported the government's argument that Sullivan's actions were planned in advance and were conducted with malicious intent. "It is highly unlikely that a programmer would recognize these lines of code as being destructive during routine code inspection or maintenance," said Repede. "Not only is there a lack of organization and a scattered placement of these code lines, but there also is a selection of names for variables that is clearly intended to disguise their purpose."[94]

For example, the logic bomb code was broken into small pieces, which were then disguised by the use of misleading variable names. Sullivan then concealed the pieces of code in 10 different procedures. Finally, the ultimate effect of the code was not to disable the printdoc.bas module itself, said Repede, but to disable another portion of the program. This served to "focus programmers' attention elsewhere after the system crashed," according to Repede. "These factors indicate a carefully planned effort to avoid detection."[95]

Sullivan's logic bomb self-detonated as planned – months after he had resigned and left the company. And when that happened, more than 700 of the 2,000 Lance sales executives became isolated from the company's headquarters for several days as they traveled around the U.S. with heaps of potato chips and crackers. Although millions of dollars in sales were immediately put at risk, the company was able to limit the damage to several hundred thousand dollars.

On April 13, 2001, U.S. District Judge Richard Voorhees sentenced Sullivan to two years in prison and fines totaling more than $194,000. Sullivan filed an appeal in the case but lost.

.. -. ... .. -.. . / .--- --- -...

The Reconnex risk assessments conducted at companies throughout the manufacturing and retail sectors uncovered a wide array of potential legal liabilities, as well as an abundance of office documents containing proprietary or secret information.

A 48-hour risk assessment conducted at a manufacturing firm in Nov.

2004, for example, not only found the usual violations, such as unprotected social security numbers, but also unsecured e-mail attachments that outlined employee payroll information with corresponding social security numbers, customer lists, purchase orders, employee disciplinary documentation, and a host of other administrative data that contained personal identifying information.

Of particular concern during the risk assessment, which was focused on outbound communications originating within the firm's engineering department, was the content of various Word and Excel files. Some contained operations and inspection reports that depicted critical information, such as the signatures of senior personnel in the engineering and management ranks, as well as company seals ("Red Stamps") that could be subject to forgery. Other data contained in numerous files included a customer invoice that outlined customer ID numbers and a campaign fulfillment list that catalogued customer names, account numbers, addresses, telephone numbers, division heads and their spouses.

As with many other companies throughout various industries, the network of this particular manufacturing firm was also laboring under the weight of an inordinate number of image files – an unlikely file format given this particular firm's business requirements. But the high volume of images was not the biggest problem; when it came to image files, the content was the biggest concern to the executives at the firm. The Reconnex iGuard system intercepted files containing images of proprietary circuit designs, nudity and adult content, and weapons. There also were numerous files containing source code that were communicated via File Transfer Protocol (FTP) without the use of encryption.

In April 2005, the manufacturer of one of the biggest brand names in the world underwent a 48-hour Reconnex risk assessment. And to its surprise, the Reconnex system noted 123 engineering and design documents leaving the network. This occurred as the company was completing the design of a new product and developing a major, new marketing campaign to support the upcoming product release.

This particular company "makes huge investments in the design, production, promotion and launch of new products every year," according to the Reconnex risk assessment report developed for this firm. "It is crucial to their business that all aspects of that process are kept confidential. The competition in [this company's} market is fierce and leakage of research and development, engineering designs, new product advertising campaign information…can be detrimental to [the company's] competitive advantage."

In addition to potentially losing proprietary design data on a major new product line, this particular company was also unaware that it may have a problem with employees leaking sensitive financial information for the purposes of insider stock trading. File Transfer Protocol (FTP) traffic – an insecure communications protocol – was discovered going to two major banks, four destinations overseas and at least 268 locations in the U.S. More important, there were 958 Web posts to stock data message boards discovered that clearly indicated the possibility that employees may have been using their access to and knowledge of the company's upcoming product launch for financial gain.

The Reconnex risk assessment report provided to this particular company noted that "if employees leak inside information onto public stock message boards using the [company's] corporate network resources, the company could be exposed to shareholder suits, SEC investigations and loss of brand reputation."

.. -. ... .. -.. . / .--- --- -...

Two major companies in the transportation industry underwent voluntary 48-hour risk assessments using the Reconnex iGuard system. Both discovered major legal liability risks and security problems.

The first company underwent a risk assessment from Nov. 14 through Nov. 16 of last year. Immediately, the system caught 184 social security numbers leaving the corporate network in clear text. The numbers were discovered in e-mail attachments as well as embedded in the text of e-mail. "This violation could be considered a material internal control weakness under the Sarbanes-Oxley Act," the Reconnex assessment report stated.

The situation of the second company, however, is more serious. This particular firm has expressed specific concern about terrorism and, to its dismay, discovered an inadvertent security leak of detailed scheduling data that could have enabled a terrorist group to cause the company great damage.

News Story

Shareholders sue ChoicePoint

The company's share price has dropped more than 20% in a month

News Story by Joris Evers

MARCH 07, 2005 (IDG NEWS SERVICE) - Shareholders are suing Choice-Point Inc. and its top executives after the company's share price fell sharply following news that identity thieves had gained access to personal information about some U.S. residents that was held by the personal data vendor.

A class-action lawsuit has been filed in U.S. District Court for the Central District of California on behalf of those who bought ChoicePoint shares between April 22, 2004, and March 3, 2005, Radnor, Pa.-based law firm Schiffrin & Barroway LLP said in a statement Friday. The suit charges Alpharetta, Ga.-based ChoicePoint and three top executives with keeping key information from the public in an effort to artificially inflate the price of the company's stock.

Specifically, the suit alleges that the defendants knew that ChoicePoint's measures to protect its data were inadequate, that the company knew it was selling data to illegal enterprises, that security breaches had occurred twice before and that the company had exposed more than 500,000 people to the threat of identity theft.

The suit seeks to recover damages for the shareholders. ChoicePoint's stock has nose-dived since the company acknowledged that it had mistakenly given personal information of U.S. residents to identity thieves. ChoicePoint shares closed at $37.65 on Friday, near its 52-week low of $37.24 and far from the $47.85 price on Feb. 4, which was near its 52-week high.

ChoicePoint has access to about 19 billion public records. The company reportedly has information on virtually every adult living in the U.S. It has been the focus of intense scrutiny and criticism since it acknowledged last month that identity thieves gained access to records and personal information on people in all 50 U.S. states, the District of Columbia, Puerto Rico, Guam and the U.S. Virgin Islands. Information provided by ChoicePoint has since been used in about 750 identity theft scams.

Since disclosing the security breach, the company has been the focus of a U.S. Federal Trade Commission inquiry into its compliance with federal information security laws, a U.S. Securities and Exchange Commission investigation into possible insider stock trading violations by its CEO and chief operating officer, and lawsuits alleging violations of the federal Fair Credit Reporting Act and California state law, ChoicePoint disclosed in a filing to the SEC on Friday.

Chapter 11

Blind Security

Healthcare & Biotech

"Science is a wonderful thing if one does not have to earn one's living at it."
– Albert Einstein

On Feb. 20, 2003, the U.S. Department of Health and Human Services (HHS) published its final rule governing the security standards that healthcare providers must adhere to for the protection of patient data. The deadline for implementing the provisions of the rule was April 20, 2005. The 289-page rule, which covers the "confidentiality, integrity and availability" of personally identifying healthcare data, is part of the 1996 Health Insurance Portability and Accountability Act (HIPAA).

But HIPAA was passed as a means to improve the transferability and accountability of health insurance by enforcing standards for electronic codes and processing of claims. Doctors, insurance companies and hospitals hate HIPAA, although it keeps patients and their money moving through the system. Likewise, security practitioners view HIPAA and its security rule as a mysterious illness with no clear treatment history from which to draw lessons.

One of the major problems with the security and privacy provisions of HIPAA has been the use of vague language that has left the rules open to a wide array of interpretations about how best to secure patient data and what the law actually requires. For example, the final published rule stops short of dictating specific security technologies or approaches that could be employed by all the affected healthcare entities. According to lawmakers, the language is deliberately vague because the U.S. healthcare system is "so varied in terms of installed technology, size, resources and relative risk." The rule further noted that many of the technology experts who commented on the rule during the public comment period "supported the concept of technological neutrality, which would afford [healthcare companies] the flexibility to select appropriate technology solutions and to adopt new technology over time."

This is the essence of the security menace that now faces the U.S. health-care industry. Whenever the government dabbles in weak language in an effort to feign determined action, the organizations that must live or die by the new laws do so at the whim of practitioners who often hold vastly different interpretations of the requirements. What is left is a hodgepodge of security standards. And the real loser is the American citizen, who never quite knows – from one hospital, doctor or insurance company to another – if their personal healthcare information is protected properly.

Despite these problems, there is a reasonable explanation for why they exist. Put simply, the U.S. healthcare industry is such a mammoth bureaucracy – one that makes the Department of Homeland Security look like a 'Mom and Pop' shop – that inaction and lack of adherence to security standards can go on for months, years or decades without coming to light. And it is precisely this type of chaotic corporate environment that gives birth to malicious insiders and legal liability problems.

.. -. ... .. -.. . / .--- --- -...

Thousands of privacy violations occur throughout the U.S. healthcare industry every year; and those are only the ones we know about. During the 10 months leading up to Feb. 28, 2005, for example, there were more than 11,280 complaints of privacy violations filed to the HHS Office for Civil Rights (OCR). And the complaints touched upon a wide variety of inappropriate privacy and security practices.

According to the HHS OCR, the top five complaints investigated during that time frame were:

(1) Impermissible disclosures (e.g., gossiping to a friend outside the hospital about the medical condition of a neighbor who is a patient);
(2) Lack of adequate safeguards (e.g., leaving files around, not protecting [patient health-care information] PHI on computer screens);
(3) Refusal or failure to provide access to — or a copy of — medical records;
(4) Disclosure of more than the minimum necessary protected health information; and
(5) Failure to include valid language in patient authorizations for PHI disclosures.

But the future of medical privacy in America is frightening. Although hospitals and healthcare providers have been slow to adopt new information technologies to enhance information sharing (due primarily to significant budget challenges), the digitization of private healthcare data is now a fact.

And that digital corpus continues to grow at an ever increasing rate. While new advances will certainly result from the improved ability of doctors, researchers and scientists to interact and share information on diseases and potential treatments, weak and confusing laws, and the lack of standards throughout the healthcare and health insurance industries means that Americans' most private information is not only at risk of compromise by somebody inside the system, but may one day be made available to those who are unscrupulous enough to use a person's medical data against them.

In fact, a Boston-based organization called the Medical Information Bureau (MIB) is the healthcare industry's equivalent of ChoicePoint. The MIB, an association of health insurance firms, stores private health data on millions of Americans and shares that data anytime somebody applies for insurance or files an insurance claim.

While the amassing of private health data is certainly a major potential problem for privacy in America, there is a new dark cloud approaching: the harvesting and a storing of DNA (Deoxyribonucleic Acid – a person's genetic blueprint). Some private DNA testing companies now claim to store tens of thousands of DNA samples, some acquired with the consent of the owner and some not.[96] And this is where the confluence of a technological surveillance society and malicious insiders could spell catastrophe for privacy in America.

The inadvertent or deliberate leak of personal DNA and other healthcare data could lead to a tidal wave of discrimination. Health insurance companies could use the information to deny those seeking insurance; employers could discriminate on the basis of a person's potential future health problems; and neighbors could one day know details about each other's medical conditions simply by searching the Web. These scenarios are all too real. And they are not primarily a technological problem; they are an insider problem.

.. -. ... .. -.. . / .--- --- -...

The worlds of economic espionage and medical privacy have also recently converged. One such case involved the targeting of research into Alzheimer's disease, a deterioration of brain tissue that affects more than 4 million people in the U.S. and approximately 15 million people worldwide.

Research into the genetic factors leading to Alzheimer's has been underway for many years at the Learner Research Institute (LRI), a part of the Cleveland Clinic Foundation (CCF) in Ohio. In January 1997, LRI hired a researcher by the name of Takashi Okamoto. His mission was to study the potential causes and treatments of Alzheimer's. And he was to accomplish this research using DNA samples and cell line reagents developed by CCF and the National Institutes of Health. But prosecutors in Ohio soon alleged that Okamoto had other plans for the DNA.

In April 1999, Okamoto received and accepted an offer to become a neuroscience researcher for the Institute of Physical and Chemical Research (RIKEN), a quasi-public corporation in Japan that received more than 94% of its funding from the Japanese Ministry of Science and Technology. Two years earlier, the Brain Science Institute of RIKEN had established a new neuroscience program to study, among other things, the possible genetic causes and treatments of Alzheimer's disease.

After having accepted his new position, Okamoto contacted a long-time friend, known only as "Dr. A." Late in the evening on July 8, 1999, the two men entered Laboratory 164 at CCF, where Okamoto worked. Once there, they packed 10 cell line reagents and DNA samples into boxes and destroyed those they did not wish to take. To cloak their activities, they filled vials with tap water and labeled them so that they would look like the missing cell line agents. Two days later, Okamoto took the boxes containing the real material and temporarily stored them at the Cleveland home of another co-conspirator and a fellow CCF employee, known only as "Dr. B."

On July 12, Okamoto picked up the boxes from Dr. B's home and mailed them to Kansas City, Kansas, and the home of Hiroaki Serizawa – a long-time friend he had met in Boston. Two weeks later, Okamoto resigned from his position at CCF and, on August 3, began his new career at RIKEN in Japan. Okamoto returned to the U.S. on August 16 for the purpose of collecting the DNA and cell line reagents from Serizawa. However, lab officials soon became aware that somebody had stolen the DNA materials after other scientists complained that the vials left by Okamoto (the vials filled with tap water) didn't work during their experiments.

On May 8, 2001, a grand jury returned a four-count indictment against both Serizawa and Okamoto. The indictment stated that Okamoto's goal was "to ensure that RIKEN acquired a competitive advantage over" U.S. scientists studying Alzheimer's disease.

Okamoto denied the charges through a lawyer in Japan. In 2002, the U.S. officially requested his extradition to face charges of economic espionage. In March 2004, however, the Tokyo High Court denied the U.S. request, arguing that Okamoto had no intention of profiting from the delivery of the samples to RIKEN and that there was not sufficient reason to suspect he had committed a crime.

Serizawa pled guilty on May 1, 2002 to one-count charging him with making false statements to the FBI during the investigation into the missing materials.

.. -. ... .. -.. . / .--- --- -...

A little more than a month later, the FBI arrested two researchers in Boston for attempting to steal proprietary biomedical trade secrets belonging to

Harvard Medical School's Department of Cell Biology. Federal prosecutors charged Jiangyu Zhu, a/k/a "Jiang Yu Zhu" and Kayoko Kimbara with attempting to sell, to a Japanese company, information pertaining to Harvard research into immunosuppressive drugs to control organ rejection, as well as genes that regulate calcineurin, an important signaling enzyme in the heart, brain and immune systems.

According to the affidavit filed in the case, both Zhu and Kimbara were working as post-doctoral research candidates under the direction of a Harvard professor. It was there, at Harvard, where the two met and later married. The research, which was funded by the National Institutes of Health and the American Cancer Society, focused on screening drugs, proteins and genes to determine which drugs might control organ rejection after transplants. Of particular concern was finding genes that might help control calcineurin, an immune cell constituent that, when activated, can cause organ transplant rejection.

By Feb. 1999, Kimbara had achieved some success, identifying two genes that encode proteins that bind to calcineurin. By Sept., the research showed even greater potential. In addition to tightly binding calcineurin, the two genes identified by Kimbara blocked the activity of calcineurin. These findings offered a potential means of treating a number of diseases affecting the immune, cardiovascular, and nervous systems and, therefore, had significant commercial potential.

However, the two researchers suddenly began working nights. They entered the secured laboratory at 11 p.m. and worked until 9 a.m. This allowed them to work without the oversight of the Harvard professor. Eventually, the professor realized that Kimbara was doing secret work that she was not sharing with him. In fact, although they reported the discovery of four genes that held promise, prosecutors alleged that the two researchers discovered at least seven additional genes. Harvard filed a provisional patent on the first two genes and their products on Oct. 22, 1999.

The Institute of Biotechnology at the University of Texas then offered Zhu a job on Dec. 13, 1999. But after receiving the job offer and while still employed at Harvard, Zhu sent an e-mail to a San Antonio-based Japanese biochemical company that outlined his intent to partner with a fellow researcher to commercialize the research he had done at Harvard. He eventually sent three new genes to the firm in Japan. The firm took those genes and produced valuable antibodies and then sent the antibodies back to Zhu.

Later that month, Zhu and Kimbara informed Harvard of their intention to take positions at the University of Texas. They were to start their new jobs on January 15, 2000. But before heading to the Lone Star state, they had some packing to do.

Between Dec. 27 and Jan. 1, they entered the Harvard Laboratory in the early morning hours and late at night. There they packed more than 30 boxes full of biological materials, books and documents for shipment to the University of Texas. The estimated value of the materials and research that Zhu and Kimbara had been working on was more than $300,000.

Harvard officials didn't notice the missing materials until Jan. 3. When questioned about it, Zhu and Kimbara denied taking anything. And while many of the materials that the two researchers allegedly stole from Harvard were eventually recovered from their office spaces at the University of Texas, some of the materials have not been recovered.

As of this writing, Zhu and Kimbara were free on $250,000 bail and awaiting trial. Some, particularly in the research community, have stated publicly that the government has overreacted to the case and, by pursuing Zhu and Kimbara so aggressively, demonstrated a complete lack of understanding of how the research community works. The author called the U.S. Attorney's office in Boston on May 9, 2005 and asked for an update on the case against the two researchers. A spokesperson said there had been no change in the status of the case and that the charges were still pending.

.. -. ... .. -.. . / .--- --- -...

The targeting of proprietary data in the biomedical industry should come as no surprise to anybody who has even briefly glanced at the market forecast for the industry. There is an undeclared guerilla war being waged around the world, the goal of which is to cripple the superpowers of the biomedical field by beating them to the market with life-saving formulas for drugs and other research. And stealing that advantage is a tactic that many are willing to employ. There is simply too much to be gained – several trillion dollars by the year 2020, to be exact.

R.P. Scherer Inc. (RPS), a St. Petersburg, Florida-based international developer of drug delivery systems that improve the efficacy of drugs by regulating their dosage, rate of release and absorption, knows exactly what's at stake and what some people are willing to do to take advantage of their access to highly-valued secrets.

In August 1999, Jolene Rector contacted a friend, Steven Snyder, who worked at RPS and requested that he send her proprietary information that would assist her in her job at a direct competitor of RPS. Snyder did exactly that, sending information on the company's gel formulas, fill formulas, shell weights, and experimental production order (EPO) data to Rector in Nevada, where she was working at the time.

A few weeks later, Rector initiated a conversation with the production manager of Nelson Paint Ball, Inc. (NPB), located in Kingsford, Michigan. Among the many things that RPS formulas are used for are paintballs and other recreational items. Rector told the manager that she possessed gelatin formulas from R.P Scherer that she would be willing to sell for $50,000. She said she had obtained the formulas from RPS' SOFT GELCAPS WEST facility, paintball plant and nutritional plant, before she was laid-off.

On August 31, she faxed the manager at Nelson Paint Ball several pages containing gel formulas, maintenance instructions, a map of RPS' paintball facility, and a pilot plan notebook.

Within minutes of receiving the fateful fax, the product manager along with the legal counsel at Nelson Paint Ball faxed the documents back to attorneys at RPS. Rector had no idea that she had been caught in a corporate-run sting operation. Lawyers from R.P. Scherer then contacted the FBI.

On Sept. 29, the executive vice president of Nelson Paint Ball initiated a telephone call to Rector and requested that it be recorded for accuracy. Rector, obviously not the most sophisticated corporate insider to walk the earth, agreed. During the conversation, Rector said she had already sold a portion of the data to an unnamed buyer but that she would be willing to sell the remainder to Nelson Paint Ball for a mere $25,000. The executive at Nelson said he would have to get back to her with a decision.

The following day, the executive at Nelson Paint Ball called Rector a second time. Once again, the conversation was recorded with Rector's permission.

"You don't sound like you want to travel to Michigan to make this happen," the executive said.

"Yeah, well on an illegal thing no," Rector said, laughing.[97] "Because you know if I'm doing something that's not ill.., not legally put down as like I'm doing a job...Yeah, then I'm setting myself up to get caught or whatever," she said. "You know wherever I go I'm setting myself up...but if there's a contract and a job, you know a job contract, then it's not a set up it, you know I'm basically doing a legal work...because it actually has...it doesn't have nobody's name on it , it is my stuff."

When the executive from Nelson Paint Ball asked Rector what she had done with the information in the book from the pilot plant, she stated that she re-wrote it by hand and destroyed the book. She also said she was in possession of a maintenance manual for a Japanese encapsulation machine, approximately 106 gel formulas, and 60 paint ball formulas.

Rector finally agreed to a meeting with a special representative of Nelson Paint Ball who was to be sent by the company's executive vice president. The meeting took place on October 14, 1999. Rector handed the representative a maroon-colored three-ring binder. Insider was the maintenance manual she had described on the telephone, as well as the gel formulas, paintball formulas, and shell weights. In return for the binder, the company's representative handed Rector a check for $25,000.

But Rector also got something she wasn't counting on: a surprise. The company representative then informed her that he was not an employee of Nelson Paint Ball. He was an FBI agent and their meeting had just been video taped. She would plead guilty on March 13, 2001 to the charges that were eventually brought against her.

On Friday afternoon, January 25, 2002, District Court Judge James S. Moody, Jr., sentenced Rector to 14 months in prison. Steven Synder was sentenced to 10 months in prison.

.. -. ... .. -.. . / .--- --- -...

The Reconnex Risk Assessments

In Nov. 2004, Reconnex conducted a live, 48-hour risk assessment at a major biotech company. The results validate the concerns that government law enforcement officials have had for years: that America's biotech and healthcare research fields are ill with a cancer that is spreading uncontrollably and that is slowly killing innovation.

Among the most startling findings of the Reconnex risk assessment were six (6) internal e-mail messages that were sent to or received from employees at a direct competitor of the bio-tech firm. There were also 321 instances of proprietary, unencrypted source code discovered leaving the firm's network, as well as 25 engineering documents.

Once again, social security numbers were found in the body of clear-text e-mails and in e-mail attachments. This happened at least 38 times during the 48-hour risk assessment. In addition, although the company had published a security policy that forbade employees from downloading multimedia files from the Internet, the Reconnex system uncovered 92 instances of such downloads in 48 hours.

The general healthcare enterprises that underwent a Reconnex risk assessment faired no better than the above biotech research firm. A 48-hour snapshot of network activity taken at a major healthcare facility in Feb. 2005 showed at least 62 potential security policy violations. The breakdown of the policy violations discovered during the risk assessment is outlined below:

Confidential Information: 62%
Governance: 48%
HIPAA: 18%
Proprietary Data: 16%

In addition, the following outlines the items that represent the highest severity of potential security and legal liability problems:

Confidential payroll data was sent outside the organization to a personal e-mail account.

Social Security Numbers with names, addresses,
date of birth, and other identifiers were sent out
to/from the Internet in unencrypted clear text.

Examples of protected health information (PHI)
with associated medical record numbers (MRNs)
were sent to personal e-mail accounts and unknown Internet destinations.

Anomalous transfers of PHI were observed using
known network protocols and non-standard ports.

In the most recent risk assessment conducted (as of this writing) by Reconnex, technicians noted an inbound communication that included an
unencrypted spreadsheet with more than 500 patient names, dates of birth and
social security numbers. The spreadsheet was pulled in from a Yahoo mail
account. In the spreadsheet there was a column for referral information; many
of the patients were referred to AIDS clinics in the hospital's Correctional
Managed Care program.

Although this information was inbound, it is of an extremely sensitive nature and the information somehow made its way to a Yahoo mail server. The
use of personal e-mail accounts, including Yahoo, Microsoft's Hotmail, AOL
and Google's gmail, raises additional confidentiality and privacy control issues. Exposing private data such as social security numbers is a violation of
several Federal and state regulations and can create serious damage to a
hospital's reputation. In addition, the loss of confidence from patients could
further erode the healthcare facility's repute.

In February 2005, a Palm Beach County Florida employee mistakenly e-
mailed a list of approximately 6,500 HIV/AIDS patients to 800 County health
workers. Shortly thereafter some of the people on the list started receiving
mail stating that they were on a list of HIV-positive people.

This incident has sparked investigations by local and state authorities as
well as the FBI and U.S. Postal Service.

Chapter 12

The Physics of Catching Insiders

"Google is the ultimate forensics tool. But Google has the advantage of time. Our problem is much harder."
– Dr. Ratinder Ahuja, chief technical officer, Reconnex Corp.

A trip to the headquarters of Reconnex Corp. in Mountain View, California, is like entering a seminary for mad scientists. It's also a little like visiting with a bunch of NASA space engineers – in fact, NASA was critical in helping the company perfect its technologies.

When I visited the firm on several occasions last year during the course of researching this book, I was astounded by the amount of technical expertise required to create a security device capable of, for the first time, effectively addressing the insider problem. I traveled to Reconnex fully expecting to meet with standard, run-of-the-mill IT developers that are common throughout the Silicon Valley. What I experienced was something completely different. If I had to guess a company in the Valley that represents that area's concentration of Ph.D.'s (among the highest in the nation), Reconnex would be on my short list. And now, many months after first beginning my research into the insider threat and methods of battling that threat, it is no surprise to me that a company with the amount of brain power that Reconnex has behind it has finally developed insider security technology that is capable of operating in the most demanding IT environments.

.. -. ... .. -.. . / .--- --- -...

To understand the significance of what is happing inside the walls of Reconnex, we have to start with the history of one man: Don Massaro, the company's founder and CEO. A long-time veteran of the IT industry, Massaro considers himself more of a physicist than an IT engineer. And that's actually very appropriate. He studied aeronautical engineering at Notre Dame because he "wanted to build rocket engines." But after almost blowing up his family's house, he went on to graduate school at Northwestern where he earned a Master's degree in plasma physics. From Northwestern it was on to Berkeley, where Massaro pursued a doctorate degree in heat transfer and thermodynamics.

It's obvious when you talk to Massaro that you're not talking to a typical IT professional. His first job out of Berkeley was a summer gig with IBM. It was the late 1960s and computer science as a discipline did not exist yet. The region we know today as the Silicon Valley was nothing but orchards and farms. And there were no small companies to work for in those days; you either worked for IBM, Lockheed or Hewlett-Packard, or you didn't work in the computer business.

"I showed up at the IBM San Jose lab right out of Berkeley. Back then at IBM everybody wore white shirts and ties. But this lab was kind of a maverick lab. They were wearing light blue shirts," Massaro recalled with a laugh. "There I was, on the other hand, wearing a dark brown suit with black pin stripes, black shirt and a black and brown tie. There was a lottery to see how long it would be before I was called into the director's office. The guy who picked ten minutes won."

Fortunately, his visit to the director's office resulted in nothing more than being handed $200 dollars in cash and an order to go buy a few light blue shirts and a blue suit. At IBM, he was first assigned to the technology group. But unlike his Big Blue counterparts, who looked at this young kid from Berkeley with more than a little skepticism, he would never design anything on paper.

"I was more of a physicist than an engineer," Massaro recalled during a lengthy interview at his office in California. "I was always building simulation models, mathematical models to describe the process of the particular problem I was working on."

That's when IBM put him on their latest technical challenge – building floppy disk drives. Early hard disk drives developed by IBM in the 1950s used heads that were in contact with the surface of the disk. As a result, the disks would wear out over time. Massaro was given the mission of understanding how to create a floppy disk that would use a head that floated over the surface of the disk by means of an air bearing system.

With Big Blue struggling to get their current research out of the lab and into a product, Massaro went to work. Soon, he realized that the equation IBM researchers were using looked a lot like the heat transfer equations he used to work with in school. So, instead of solving for temperature Massaro decided to use the equations and solve for pressure. These were simple equations – that is, if you are a physicist.

"They were non-linear partial differential equations with three spatial variables in time," he explained during our interview. Don't ask. I didn't.

Eventually, Massaro walked into his supervisor's office with startling news.

"I think I can solve this," he said. "I just need a really big computer."

Well, he was in the right place. IBM had plenty of "big" computers.

He was given an IBM 360 Mod 75 to work with. At the time, this system represented major computing power. Today, it probably has less computing power than a digital camera. It took him three weeks to write the simulations via punch cards. It then took the IBM 360 two hours to simulate one half of a revolution of the disk, which in real time took 8 milliseconds. By today's standards, it was a long, arduous process. But it worked.

By 1969, people were starting to leave the IBM lab and start their own companies. It was the beginning of the Silicon Valley as it is known today. One of the first executives to leave Big Blue was Al Shugart, the former assistant lab manager. He had been recruited by Memorex to put Memorex in the disk drive business. He then picked a handful of key technologists to come to Memorex with him. Among these key technologists, who became known throughout the industry as the IBM Dirty Dozen, was Don Massaro.

At Memorex, Massaro led the engineering team. During his time there, Memorex had produced a great disk drive product – one that Massaro now thinks was actually better than what IBM had been producing. But Memorex was beginning to consider the possibility of taking on IBM in the mainframe business – a road littered with the corpses of failed companies that did not understand the power of IBM in the mainframe market. By the end of 1971, the situation at Memorex was bad enough to convince Al Shugart to leave and venture out on his own.

In 1972, Shugart came up with an idea to start a low-cost hard drive business. And Massaro is there. Thus, Shugart Associates is born, with Massaro as vice president of engineering and manufacturing. Within a few years, Massaro is CEO and on his way to becoming a multi-millionaire. And he's not yet 30 years old.

The company started out developing the 8-inch floppy disk drive, which now sits in the Smithsonian Institute. Then they turned their attention to the 5 ¼ inch drive. And Massaro begins to ask the same questions he asked at IBM.

"Why can't we take the mechanics of a floppy and make a hard disk out of it?" asked Massaro.

At that time, hard disks were very expensive. Nobody believed it was possible to shrink the form factor and lower the price tag. But Massaro was convinced all that was necessary was finding a way to compensate for the heat expansion of the disk. Once again, he turns to his physics and simulation experience to prove that a low-cost hard drive was possible.

He decides to design a base plate out of aluminum that has the same expansion characteristics of the disk. His theory is simple: one will off-set the other. It worked. In 1977 Shugart brought to the market a hard disk drive that had a 14-inch disk in it but with all the mechanics of a floppy. They sold it for $1,000. That was Shugart's great and enduring contribution to the IT industry. But they never got full credit. Shugart was acquired by Xerox.

By 1979, Massaro found himself at Xerox Corp., heading up the company's Office Products Division. It took only one visit to Xerox' Palo Alto Research Center (PARC) for Massaro to see the future of computing.

"I almost had a heart-attack," he recalled. "What I saw was ALTOS, the first iconic computer. And it was on a local area network called the Ethernet. And they were doing laser printing. And the desktop of the ALTOS had icons and you moved them around with a device called a mouse. This is it, I said."

And he was right. The $40 million a year that Xerox had pumped into the PARC had produced much of the desktop technology that the world takes for granted today: desktop icons, the mouse, electronic printing, e-mail, and the client-server architecture.

Massaro announced the first iconic computer at the first national computer show. And every Xerox presentation at that trade show had one thing in common – Steve Jobs was sitting in the front row. Massaro had known Jobs previously because the legendary co-founder of Apple Computer Inc. was among the biggest customers of the mini-floppy disk drive.

"When I got back to my office from that trade show I had a bouquet of flowers waiting for me from Steve Jobs. He thanked me for bringing the technology to the market. Jobs then came out with Lisa, which led to the Macintosh. The rest, as they say, is history."

In his 18 months at Xerox, Massaro brought 7 new products to the market, destroying the typical Xerox product cycle of 7 years.

But the politics at Xerox was stifling and distracting. And Massaro admits now that his rebel-like, unconventional leadership style didn't help the situation.

"Don was the opposite of everything the corporate staff culture respected," said John Titsworth, a former member of the Xerox board of directors. "The staff was dignified, quiet, bureaucratic, protective, cautious, staff-dependent, politically-oriented and stuffed shirts. He was flashy, boisterous, entrepreneurial, open, 'full speed ahead', decisive, and couldn't care less about politics."

It was that entrepreneurial spirit and honesty that would sabotage Massaro's chance at taking the reins at Xerox. He eventually walked out of one of the executive board meetings never to return. From there, he decided to run companies his way, to push the technological envelope and, if he could, find a way to serve the greater good.

.. -. ... .. -.. . / .--- --- -...

Reconnex Corp. is Massaro's fifth company and the one he is, arguably, most proud of. It is the incarnation of his desire to push technology to its limits and serve the greater good during an increasingly dangerous time for the country. At staff meetings, he makes a point to remind his engineers that "they are on the side of the angels" when it comes to the work they are doing at Reconnex.

The research and development taking place at Reconnex is truly unique. But it is the expertise that Massaro has gathered around him that is critical to the company's technical success to date.

Rick Lowe is the company's Vice President of Engineering and drives the development and testing of all products. With more than 20 years of experience, Lowe's resume includes a stint as a development manager at Cisco Systems, where he played a significant role in helping to develop multiservice ATM switching technologies and bring the Cisco PIX firewall to the market.

When I asked Lowe to describe the factors that make the Reconnex iGuard system different from the horde of other products that are on the market, his answer was surprisingly low-tech, yet straight to the point.

"If you're standing at a crosswalk and counting the cars that go by, does that give you any insight into what's inside those cars?" asked Lowe, rhetorically. "Does that give you any insight into why those cars are driving down that road? Or insight into why they are going the speed they are going?"

The answer, obviously, is no. But from an insider security perspective, "Reconnex can tell you what's inside that car," said Lowe. "And from that information you'll likely get a very good idea why they are traveling down that particular road."

What Lowe is talking about is truly revolutionary in the world of security, especially when it comes to monitoring insider abuse. The technology has resulted in the first information security appliance to offer real-time content analysis at blazing gigabit network speeds. Without exception, the companies and government agencies that have been exposed to the technology during the company's 48-hour risk assessments have watched in awe as the system's real-time content processing engine (RCPE) captures, classifies, reconstructs, and stores files and documents of all types. It is a capability that had until today not existed and it is changing the face of insider security and regulatory compliance.

Massaro expects to "own the market" by capturing two-thirds of the business in insider threat monitoring. And he doesn't plan on out-marketing the competition. To the contrary, he plans to grow the business through engineering and physics.

"We solved the physics problem" that had been preventing companies and agencies from attaining this type of visibility into what is going on inside their enterprises, he said. And it is no surprise that it was Reconnex that solved the physics problem. In addition to Massaro, the company counts among its engineers several Ph.D.s and a former scientist with the Los Alamos National Laboratory.

But what does Massaro mean when he talks about physics and the challenge of identifying and stopping insider abuse? The best way to describe the answer to that question is to consider what the actual technical challenge was that confronted the Reconnex engineers. A network, for example, at any given time might have more than 100,000 "sessions," or application conversations, taking place. Some employees might be sending e-mail, others might be surfing the Internet, and still others might be sharing documents of all types. And, to make matters worse, the packets of data that make up these sessions are completely random – they leave and return to the network in random order and must be reconstructed for the data to make sense to the user.

To analyze such a chaotic environment – and one where the data is moving at gigabit speeds (1,024 megabits or approximately 1 billion bits per second) – it is necessary for the security device to be able to pull the data off the network, reconstruct the session, analyze it, find the object (Word documents, Powerpoint presentations, Web sessions, e-mail, etc...), analyze the object to determine if there is any content present that indicates a security threat, and, if there is such data present, write the data to a disk for storage and forensic analysis.

Reconnex's chief technical officer and co-founder, Dr. Ratinder Paul Singh Ahuja, had been working on overcoming the physics problem involved in this level of insider monitoring and forensics capability for quite some time when he met Massaro. The two had approached the same venture capital firm and, when they realized they had the same idea for an insider monitoring company and technology, conducted a bloodless merger before there was even a company.

In many ways, Ahuja is the driving force behind the company's technology accomplishments. But getting to where they are today was not easy, he said.

There were four performance thresholds that Ahuja had to overcome during the development process. The first challenge was finding a way to handle blazing network data rates – a challenge that has crushed many other products in the security market. To do this required highly specialized work at the hardware level to improve data packet reception.

The next critical challenge was to be able to capture the content as it flew across the network at mind-bending speed and flag it for analysis. It was necessary for Ahuja and his engineers to find a way to parse more than 150 different content types in real-time while at the same time extracting information from these objects as they flew by on the network. Ahuja explains:

"Think about Google. Google is the ultimate forensics tool. But Google has the advantage of time. It takes it a month or so to gather the next set of information and make it available," Ahuja explained. "Our problem is much harder. The information is going by at very high speeds and we don't have the luxury of time."

Until Reconnex's engineers tackled the network performance challenge, it was only possible for the security industry to handle 30 megabits per second. Even on file servers running the Linux operating system, which has very good data rate handling capability. "If you take those file servers and import millions of files into a directory, all of a sudden the Linux server comes to a halt," said Ahuja. "And while the average company could never create millions of files per day, if you are sitting on the edge of a network, like our technology, and you are monitoring transactions, then it does reach the level of millions per day."

It would take Reconnex a year to solve the gigabit challenge. But they would get lucky in the process.

NASA had been looking for a technology to monitor its networks for years. And when a NASA security engineer walked into the Reconnex offices one day, the foundation was laid for Reconnex to take advantage of what amounted to the most demanding network proving ground in the world. And for Massaro, the appearance of NASA on the scene seemed like destiny.

"In order to build a high performance car, you need a race track to test it," said Massaro. And there was no faster race track in existence than the network NASA. Until that time nearly every product that NASA had tested on their massive network collapsed under the weight of unprecedented data rates. According to Ahuja, the network at a single NASA location moves more than 10 million object types in a single day.

From there, however, it was necessary to focus on offering a forensics capability to go back in time and analyze what has taken place on the network. This is the most innovative aspect of the Reconnex technology. "That required a very fast and scalable data storage and database to go along with the rest of the system," said Ahuja. "To make a cost-effective storage solution that can operate at the most demanding speeds imaginable is very difficult to do."

With NASA's help, Reconnex engineers made some fascinating, and critical, discoveries. The Reconnex system could capture data at a gigabit per second. It also could assemble and analyze the data at a gigabit per second. But it couldn't write to the disk at a gigabit per second. And that was critical to the company's ability to deliver on its forensics promise. The engineers went back to work.

The fourth and final wall that the system hit was the storage rate capability, which initially topped out at 200 megabits per second for writing captured data to the disk. The answer, however, would come partially from NASA. Engineers at the agency helped the company develop a proprietary file system – now known as the Reconnex File System (RFS) – that could store data not a 1 gigabit per second, but 1.2 gigabits per second.

Ahuja and his engineers invented what he calls a streaming file server that can record streams of data packets as they are entering the system, as opposed to individual packets of data. But when working with streams of data it is nearly impossible to make sense of the information. But by leveraging the capabilities of their data storage technology, they discovered that it was possible to know where individual elements of data were located in the massive stream.

Ahuja developed a Meta-tag scheme that would allow any organization to define up to 128 attributes of "data of interest" that could be placed into the Meta-tag on the fly – in real time. As a result, the system was now capable of producing a summary of everything that happened on the network. For the user, this was a major breakthrough in capability. Even at the end of the work day, the unique digital signature of the data that had crossed the network was still present. The system had captured and indexed everything using Meta-tag information and made that data available for ad-hoc, instantaneous forensics analysis. Now it was possible to tell the system to check off any data packets that, for example, contained social security numbers, classified project names, or any other sensitive data that executives were concerned about protecting. And if security officials were concerned about the accuracy of their search criteria, they could be changed at any time. The data that had traversed the network would still be available for analysis.

It seemed as if Massaro's scientists, with a little help from their fellow explorers at NASA, had struck gold while mining for copper. Data that had historically required a rack full of computers was now flowing through a single device.

Ahuja, whose led several of his own companies and is a former development manager at Cisco Systems, said he views the development of Reconnex's proprietary technology as an industry mega-trend. "Routers, firewalls, intrusion detection systems, antivirus and anti-span software, all were mega-trends," he said in an interview last year. "Now, with the technology to combat the insider threat at these network speeds, a new mega-trend is upon us."

And he may be right. The future holds many more possibilities. Paper documents, the bane of security professionals everywhere (as we've seen in the historical examples of Aldrich Ames, Jonathan Pollard and others), will one day be equipped with radio frequency identification (RFID) chips. Then, when the next Ames or Pollard prints out reams of classified documents and attempts to walk out of their office, the RFID chip will send a signal across the network wire and to the Reconnex technology, which will then immediately analyze the content and issue a security alert, if necessary.

For the first time, the technology exists to know exactly what data is entering and leaving an enterprise's network. And, more important, security officials can now conduct detailed forensics investigations on all the data that has traveled across their network. What started as a physics challenge has been chiseled by Massaro's leadership and a year-long engineering revolution into an information technology weapon system that can be used to combat the one security threat that policies and procedures alone are incapable of stopping: the insider.

Appendix A

10 Questions Every CEO
Should Be Able To Answer

The insider threat today is, believe it or not, about much more than the security of your enterprise's data. It's also about knowing that your organization has developed the right policies and procedures to prevent inadvertent disclosures or blatant misuse of corporate computer resources from becoming a hole filled with legal quicksand.

Today's regulatory environment is such that the stars are perfectly aligned for an example to be made of somebody – a company or government agency. And whomever the unfortunate soul is who sits atop the corporate chain of command at that time, he or she will wish they had taken the time to answer the following ten questions and implement the appropriate changes in their organization.

Question 1. What types of information must be protected by internal controls according to Sarbanes-Oxley?

Answer: Information should be considered nonpublic if it isn't widely disseminated to the general public, including electronic information. Unauthorized disclosure of nonpublic data is a violation of federal securities laws. This information should be protected, but it should also be monitored to ensure it isn't disclosed inappropriately.

Section 404 describes management's responsibility for building internal controls around the safeguarding of assets related to the timely detection of unauthorized acquisition, use or disposition of an entity's assets that could have a material effect on the financial statements. You need to demonstrate that you have the capabilities to monitor, detect and record electronic information disclosures.

Question 2. Since so much nonpublic information is communicated beyond e-mail based on the Simple Mail Transfer Protocol, how can we build internal controls to adequately detect the timely disclosure of information flowing over Web mail, chat, or HTTP?

Answer: In today's networked world, it's not just about e-mail. Management can't ensure the truthfulness or accuracy of financial data if it doesn't have the means to monitor the movement of sensitive information across the entire corporate network 24 hours a day, seven days a week.

Demand more from technology. New products are available that can monitor electronic disclosure of nonpublic information and aren't limited to SMTP-based e-mail. These technologies can monitor, record and provide alerts on electronic disclosures by analyzing all information flowing over the corporate network from Web mail and chat to file transfer protocol and HTTP. This type of monitoring technology combined with a storage system that allows forensic searches into stored information can prove invaluable if an investigation is required.

Question 3. What are the penalties for exposing nonpublic information?

Answer: The use of nonpublic information concerning a company or any of its affiliates (a.k.a. "inside information") in securities transactions ("insider trading"), may violate federal securities laws. Penalties can include:
- Exposure to investigations by the SEC.
- Criminal and civil prosecution.
- Relinquishing profits realized or losses avoided through use of the information.
- Penalties up to $1 million or three times the amount of any profits or losses, whichever is greater.
- Prison terms of up to 10 years.

Question 4. What action should a company take if nonpublic information is inappropriately exposed on its network?

Answer: If nonpublic information is inappropriately disclosed on your network, you must rapidly execute a response program to identify the extent of the exposure, assess the effect on the corporation and its customers, and notify all affected parties.

Section 409 of Sarbanes-Oxley mandates that companies publicly disclose additional information concerning material changes in the company's financial condition or operations. While Sarbanes-Oxley contains many reporting requirements, real-time identification of material changes and disclosures (the consensus being 48 hours) is the most significant challenge.

Question 5. Who is personally liable if there is a compliance violation?

Answer: The CEO and the CFO must certify all financial statements filed with the SEC. The maximum penalty for Securities Exchange Act violations has increased to $5 million for individuals and $25 million for entities, as well as imprisonment of up to 20 years.

Section 802 of Sarbanes-Oxley states, "Whoever knowingly alters, destroys, mutilates, conceals, covers up, falsifies, or makes a false entry in any records, documents, or tangible object with the intent to impede, obstruct, or influence the investigation or proper administration of any department or agency of the U.S. ... or contemplation of any such matter or case, shall be fined ... imprisoned not more than 20 years, or both."

Question 6. How long is the "reach back" on compliance violations?

Answer: Section 804 of Sarbanes-Oxley extends the statute of limitations in private securities fraud actions to the earlier of two years after the discovery of the facts constituting the violation or five years from the violation.

Question 7. Are there compliance strategies I can deploy to help prove due diligence if our company is investigated?

Answer: Today, an offensive rather than a defensive compliance program is important.
Deploy strategies that provide you with the evidentiary support you need when things go wrong. New network security appliances designed to capture and record all electronic communication can provide forensic capabilities with automated reporting that corresponds to compliance needs.

These solutions must be deployed within an overarching compliance strategy that aligns with the business to continuously:
- Identify and monitor risks.
- Establish effective internal controls.
- Test the validity of the controls.
- Support CEO and CFO certifications.
- Conduct third-party audits.
- Monitor for changes in risks, controls and compliance needs.
- Adjust proactively, as needed.

Question 8. What role should external auditors play in compliance?

Answer: The Public Company Accounting Oversight Board was created through the Sarbanes-Oxley Act to oversee the auditors of public companies. The board recently approved Auditing Standard No. 2, an audit of internal control over financial reporting conducted with an audit of financial statements. The new standard highlights the benefits of strong internal controls over financial reporting and furthers the objectives of Sarbanes-Oxley.

Question 9. Will I need to prevent electronic disclosures from occurring?

Answer: No compliance program can ever prevent 100% of misconduct by corporate employees. Nor do the regulations state that you must prevent internal disclosures --including electronic disclosures -- from happening.

If investigated, you will need to show due diligence that you have the ability for an appropriate and rapid response to detect and deter misconduct that exposes your company to operational risk that may have a material effect on your business.

Question 10. What happens if I am investigated?

Answer: Compliance programs should be designed to detect the particular types of operational risks most likely to occur in a corporation's lines of business. Management must be able to answer two fundamental questions:
1. Is the corporation's compliance program well-designed?
2. Does the corporation's compliance program work?

Appendix B

The Laws of Insiders

Trade Secret Offenses

18 U.S.C. 1831

§ 1831. Economic Espionage
(a) In general.--Whoever, intending or knowing that the offense will benefit any foreign government, foreign instrumentality, or foreign agent, knowingly--
(1) steals, or without authorization appropriates, takes, carries away, or conceals, or by fraud, artifice, or deception obtains a trade secret;
(2) without authorization copies, duplicates, sketches, draws, photographs, downloads, uploads, alters, destroys, photocopies, replicates, transmits, delivers, sends, mails, communicates, or conveys a trade secret;
(3) receives, buys, or possesses a trade secret, knowing the same to have been stolen or appropriated, obtained, or converted without authorization;
(4) attempts to commit any offense described in any of paragraphs (1) through (3); or
(5) conspires with one or more other persons to commit any offense described in any of paragraphs (1) through (3), and one or more of such persons do any act to effect the object of the conspiracy,
shall, except as provided in subsection (b), be fined not more than $500,000 or imprisoned not more than 15 years, or both.
(b) Organizations.--Any organization that commits any offense described in subsection (a) shall be fined not more than $10,000,000.

§ 1832. Theft of Trade Secrets
(a) Whoever, with intent to convert a trade secret, that is related to or included in a product that is produced for or placed in interstate or foreign commerce, to the economic benefit of anyone other than the owner thereof, and intending or knowing that the offense will injure any owner of that trade secret, knowingly--
(1) steals, or without authorization appropriates, takes, carries away, or conceals, or by fraud, artifice, or deception obtains such information;

(2) without authorization copies, duplicates, sketches, draws, photographs, downloads, uploads, alters, destroys, photocopies, replicates, transmits, delivers, sends, mails, communicates, or conveys such information;

(3) receives, buys, or possesses such information, knowing the same to have been stolen or appropriated, obtained, or converted without authorization;

(4) attempts to commit any offense described in paragraphs (1) through (3); or

(5) conspires with one or more other persons to commit any offense described in paragraphs (1) through (3), and one or more of such persons do any act to effect the object of the conspiracy, shall, except as provided in subsection (b), be fined under this title or imprisoned not more than 10 years, or both.

(b) Any organization that commits any offense described in subsection (a) shall be fined not more than $5,000,000.

§ 1343. Fraud by Wire, Radio, or Television

Whoever, having devised or intending to devise any scheme or artifice to defraud, or for obtaining money or property by means of false or fraudulent pretenses, representations, or promises, transmits or causes to be transmitted by means of wire, radio, or television communication in interstate or foreign commerce, any writings, signs, signals, pictures, or sounds for the purpose of executing such scheme or artifice, shall be fined under this title or imprisoned not more than five years, or both. If the violation affects a financial institution, such person shall be fined not more than $1,000,000 or imprisoned not more than 30 years, or both.

Sarbanes-Oxley Act of 2002[98]

Starting in 2004 (in the aftermath of the accounting scandals at Enron, WorldCom, Global Crossing, Tyco and Arthur Andersen), all public companies are required to submit an annual assessment of the effectiveness of their internal financial auditing controls to the Securities and Exchange Commission (SEC). In addition, each company's external auditors are required to audit and report on the internal control reports of management, in addition to the company's financial statements.

Section 302 - Certification of Annual & Quarterly Reports

CEO and CFO must review all financial reports.

Financial report does not contain any misrepresentations.

Information in the financial report is "fairly presented".

CEO and CFO are responsible for the internal accounting controls.

CEO and CFO must report any deficiencies in internal accounting controls, or any fraud involving the management of the audit committee.

CEO and CFO must indicate any material changes in internal accounting controls.

Section 404(a) - Internal Control Reports
All annual financial reports must include an Internal Control Report stating that management is responsible for an adequate internal control structure, and an assessment by management of the effectiveness of the control structure. Any shortcomings in these controls must also be reported.

Section 404(b)- External Auditor Attestation
Registered external auditors must attest to the accuracy of the company management's claim that internal accounting controls are in place, operational and effective.

Section 409 - Real-Time Disclosure
Companies are required to disclose "on a rapid and current basis such additional information concerning material changes in its financial condition or operations." In addition, it is a crime for any person to alter, destroy, or conceal any document with the intent to undermine the document's integrity or availability for use in an official proceeding.

Gramm-Leach-Bliley Act of 1999[99]
The Act repeals the 66-year old Glass-Steagall Act, which prohibited banks, securities firms and insurance companies from affiliating.

Key provisions:

Affiliation: The Act permits banks, securities firms, and insurance companies to affiliate within a new financial holding company ("FHC") structure. The Act prohibits non-financial companies from owning commercial banks.

Financial in Nature: The Act includes a broad definition of financial in nature and gives the Federal Reserve Board ("Board") the authority to define additional activities as "financial in nature, or incidental or complementary to" financial activities. Merchant banking is included in the definition of a financial activity.

Commercial Basket: The Act includes a grandfather provision for commercial activities which permits a securities firm that becomes a FHC to continue to engage in commercial activities in an amount not to exceed 15 percent of its consolidated annual gross revenues, excluding bank subsidiaries. The grandfather provision will expire ten years after date of enactment, unless extended by the Board for an additional five years.

Privacy: The Act requires all financial institutions, regardless of whether they form an FHC, to disclose to customers their policies and practices for protecting the privacy of non-public personal information. The disclosure which customers would receive at the time of establishing the relationship and at least annually thereafter would allow customers to "opt-out" of information sharing arrangements to non-affiliated third-parties. The Act permits financial institutions to share personal customer information with affiliates within the holding company. Effective immediately, it is a criminal offense for any person (including firm employees) to obtain or attempt to attain customer information relating to another person from any financial institution by making a false or fraudulent statement to an employee of that financial institution. Regulators have six months after the date of enactment to adopt final rules implementing the privacy provisions.

Requirements Regarding Financial Institution Information Practices[100]
Subtitle A establishes a framework to protect nonpublic personal information by financial institutions. There are two principal operative provisions of Subtitle V.

Section 503 generally requires that at the time a customer relationship is established and at least annually thereafter during the continuation of such relationship, a financial institution must provide a notice to consumers that describes the financial institution's policies and practices with respect to (i) disclosing nonpublic information to affiliates and nonaffiliated parties, including the categories of information that may be disclosed; (ii) disclosing nonpublic personal information of persons who are no longer customers of the financial institution, and (iii) protecting the nonpublic personal information of consumers.

Section 502 generally requires that a financial institution may not, directly or indirectly, or through any affiliate, disclose to a nonaffiliated third party any nonpublic personal information, unless (i) the institution has provided the consumer with a notice complying with the privacy policy requirements under section 503 and the institution discloses to a consumer that such information may be disclosed to a third party, (ii) the consumer is given the opportunity before the information is disclosed to direct that such information not be disclosed to such third party, and (iii) the consumer is given an explanation of how the consumer can exercise the nondisclosure option. The regulations that implement the requirements of sections 503 and 502 are discussed below.

Subtitle A also contains a series of other provisions to implement sections 503 and 502 and otherwise address the protection of nonpublic personal information by financial institutions.

California S.B. 1386 Privacy Law
California's S.B. 1386 went into effect on July 1, 2003 and is one of the most far-reaching pieces of privacy legislation in the country.

The law requires all agencies, persons or businesses that conduct business in California to notify all residents of any breach of security that resulted in the potential compromise of that resident's unencrypted personal data.

The confidentiality of personal, private data can be breached by a wide variety of incidents, including: intentional or unintentional misdirection of data; unauthorized access to data; viruses; hacking incidents; unlawful retention of data; etc...

NOTES

[1] Harrington, S.J., "The Effect of Codes of Ethics and Personal Denial of Responsibility on Computer Abuse Judgments and Intentions, *MIS Quarterly*, 20, 3, 257-278.

[2] Cited in Andrew Tobias' *Fire And Ice: The Story of Charles Revson – the Man Who Built the Revlon Empire* (William Morrow & Co, 1976), chapter 18
<http://www.andrewtobias.com/fireandice18.html>

[3] According to Tobias' account, only four "trusted" employees received the memo and Revson's FBI-trained security director could not uncover the source of the leak.

[4] Ibid.

[5] Ibid. Chapter 14 <http://www.andrewtobias.com/fireandice14.html>

[6] Ibid.

[7] Ibid.

[8] The use of electronic bugging devices is nothing new in the annals of international espionage. In fact, it is a technique that the Soviet Union and Former Soviet Union (Russia) have continued to rely upon. In Dec. 1999, for example, security officials at the State Department discovered a Russian listening device attached to the arm of a chair located in a conference room used by then-Secretary of State Madeleine Albright. The device was monitored by Stanislav Gusev, a Russian Embassy employee, from a car parked outside the headquarters facility.

[9] Neary, John, "The Big Snoop," Life Magazine, May 30, 1966.

[10] Several printed accounts, including those provided to members of Congress, allege that almost immediately upon starting work at the NCIS Pollard unexpectedly and without reason mailed classified documents to friends, and also had a problem with drugs.

[11] Ed Warner, "The Pollard Case," Voice of America Background Report, January 18, 1999.

[12] Such an evaluation is usually considered a career "death sentence" for case officers.

[13] An Assessment of the Aldrich H. Ames Espionage Case and Its Implications for U.S. Intelligence, Senate Select Committee on Intelligence, November 1, 1994.

[14] Ibid.

[15] The CIA believed the two double agents to be Soviet "controlled" double agents. Therefore, Ames believed he was passing the Soviets useless information.

[16] Interview with Ames cited in *An Assessment of the Aldrich H. Ames Espionage Case and Its Implications for U.S. Intelligence*, Senate Select Committee on Intelligence, November 1, 1994.

[17] Ibid.

[18] Heuer, Richard. "The Insider Espionage Threat," published summary of the Computer Science and Telecommunications Board, National Research Council Meeting of November 1-2, 2000 on *Cyber Security and the Insider Threat to Classified Information*, Washington, D.C.

[19] Ibid. Page 90.

[20] Ibid. Page 92.

[21] For Pollard, press and legal reports indicate the trigger may have been drug use and the need to support a habit. For Ames, the trigger seems to have been a combination of professional and personal crises that led to a lackluster career and dire financial conditions.

[22] Cited in Office of the National Counterintelligence Executive, "Annual Report to Congress on Foreign Economic Collection Industrial Espionage, 2003," February 2004, p. 1.

[23] Cited in minutes of House floor debate on Senate Intelligence Authorization Act For Fiscal Year 1995, August 12, 1994.

[24] Ibid.

[25] David E. Cooper, "Economic Espionage: Information on Threat From U.S. Allies," testimony before the Senate Select Committee on Intelligence, Feb. 28, 1996, pp. 3-4.

[26] Ibid. p. 4.

[27] Ibid. p. 5.

[28] Ibid. p. 6.

[29] Office of the National Counterintelligence Executive, Annual Report to Congress on Foreign Economic Collection Industrial Espionage, 2003, February 2004.

[30] Ibid. p. 1.

[31] Ibid. pp. v-vi.

[32] Statement by Nicholas Eftimiades, Author, "Chinese Intelligence Operations," before the Joint Economic Committee, United States Congress, May 20, 1998.

[33] Margaret Johnston, "Business spy threat is real, former CIA chief says," IDG News Service, Oct. 17, 2000.

[34] U.S. Department of Justice Press Release dated April 26, 2001.

[35] United States of America V. Yan Ming Shan, United States District Court Northern District of California, Sept. 18, 2002, p. 4.

[36] U.S. Department of Justice, "Lucent Scientists Arrested, Charged with Stealing Tech Secrets for Joint Venture with China-controlled Company," May 3, 2001.

[37] United States of America V. Fei Ye and Ming Zhong, U.S. District Court, Northern District of California, San Jose Division, Dec. 4, 2002, p. 3.

[38] Ibid.

[39] Ben McClure, "The Hidden Value of Intangibles," Investopedia.com, Dec. 16, 2004,
<http://www.investopedia.com/printable.asp?a=/articles/03/010603.asp>

[40] Baruch Lev, *Intangibles: Management, Measurement, and Reporting* (Washington: The Brookings Institution, 2001), p. 8.

[41] Ibid. p. 63

[42] American Society for Industrial Security, "Trends In Proprietary Information Loss," Survey Report, September 2002.

[43] Ibid., p. 1.

[44] The summary of the case offered here is taken from United States of America v. Timothy Lloyd, United States District Court for the District of New Jersey, April 19, 2001.

[45] Lori K. Leonard and Timothy Paul Cronan, "Illegal, Inappropriate, and Unethical Behavior in an Information Technology Context: A Study to Explain Influences," Journal of the Association of Information Systems, Feb. 2001, p. 11.

[46] Ibid. p. 21.

[47] Matt O'Connor, "FAA worker gets a year in code theft," Chicago Tribune, June 13, 2001, p. 10.

[48] Robert Baird, "Former worker ordered to prison," Pittsburgh Tribune Review, Dec. 3, 2003.

[49] "Outsourcing and the Global Marketplace: Gambling with the Health of the U.S. Economy?" The Royal Forum online,
http://www.royalforum.com/article.php?id=59

[50] Christopher Koch, "Back lash," CIO Magazine, Feb. 9, 2003.

[51] See www.tpi.net

[52] See Pete Engardio and Bruce Einhorn, "Outsourcing Innovation," BusinessWeek, March 21, 2005, pp. 84-94.

[53] Ibid.

[54] Glenn R. Jackson, "Enron and the H-1B American Worker Replacement Program: The Corporate Scandal You Are Not Hearing About," available online
<http://www.cwalocal4250.org/outsourcing/binarydata/Corporate%20Scandal.pdf>

[55] "Outsourcing and the Global Marketplace: Gambling with the Health of the U.S. Economy?" The Royal Forum online, http://www.royalforum.com/article.php?id=59

[56] CIO Magazine, Comments, Sept. 1, 2003, http://comment.cio.com/comments/13671.html.

[57] Ibid.

[58] Ibid.

[59] Ibid.

[60] The KGB (Komitet Gosudarstvenoy Bezopasnosti, or Committee For State Security) was the intelligence service of the Former Soviet Union.

[61] Martynov was a KGB Line X (technical) officer assigned to the Soviet embassy in Washington. Recruited by the FBI to serve as an agent-in-place, Martynov was eventually compromised by Aldrich Ames four months before the delivery of this anonymous letter. The Soviets recalled Martynov and executed him. Motorin and Yuzhin were also KGB Line officers in the U.S. They too were first compromised by Ames. Motorin was arrested in Moscow and executed. Yuzhin was sentenced to 15 years in prison.

[62] Victor Cherkashin, *Spy Handler: Memoir of a KGB Officer* (New York: Basic Books, 2005), p.231.

[63] In his memoir, *Spy Handler: Memoir of a KGB Officer,* Cherkashin hints that the name Fefelov may have been a cover.

[64] Federal Agency for Government Communications & Information – Federal'naya Agenstvo Pravitel'stvennoy Svayazi i Informatsii (FAPSI) – the equivalent of the U.S. National Security Agency.

[65] SVR – Sluzhhba Vneshney Razvedki Rossii, or Russian Foreign Intelligence Service, the successor of the Soviet KGB.

[66] United States of America V. Robert Phillip Hanssen, Affidavit in Support of Criminal Complaint, Arrest Warrant and Search Warrants, U.S. District Court, Eastern District of Virginia, pp. 87-88.

[67] Ibid. pp. 88-90.

[68] Victor Cherkashin, *Spy Handler: Memoir of a KGB Officer*(New York: Basic Books, 2005), p. 245.

[69] This aspect of Hanssen's psychological makeup is discussed in Cherkashin's memoir and is in stark contrast to the official characterization of Hanssen by the U.S. Government.

[70] U.S. Department of Justice Office of the Inspector General, *A Review of the FBI's Performance in Deterring, Detecting, and Investigating the Espionage Activities of Robert Philip Hanssen,* August, 2003, p.4.

[71] Ibid., p. 5.

[72] Ibid., p. 6.

[73] Ibid., p. 7.

[74] U.S. Department of Justice Commission for Review of FBI Security Programs, *A Review of FBI Security Programs,* March 31, 2002, p. 4.

[75] Ibid., p. 6.

[76] Ibid., pp. 12-26.

[77] Indictments are not proof of guilt. All defendants mentioned in this text as having been indicted on charges are presumed innocent until proven guilty. Indictment details are provided by the Department of Justice Computer Crime and Intellectual Property Section (CCIPS), http://www.usdoj.gov/criminal/cybercrime/cccases.html

[78] Steven A. McCoy, Affidavit In Support Criminal Complaint, Arrest Warrant and Search Warrants," Federal Bureau of Investigation, p. 11.

[79] Bill Miller and Walter Pincus, "Defense Analyst Accused of Spying For Cuba," Washington Post, September 22, 2001, p A1.

[80] Insider Threat Study: Illicit Cyber Activity in the Banking and Finance Sector, U.S. Secret Service and Carnegie Mellon Software Engineering Institute, August 2004.

[81] Karen Kresbach, "Security: The Inside Job," U.S. Banker, September 2004.

[82] National White Collar Crime Center Issue Paper, "Embezzlement/Employee Theft," Sept. 2002, p. 2.

[83] Sandy Haantz, "Women and White Collar Crime," National White Collar Crime Research Center, p. 1.

[84] Ibid. p 9.

[85] Ibid., p. 6.

[86] The author spent many hours searching and independently confirming the content of the Enron emails using the FERC database.

[87] Roger Matus and Sean True, "Monsters In Your Inbox: Email Liability, Compliance, and Policy Management Risk; A Case Study of the Enron Corporation," p. 5.

[88] Author Interview, March 2005, Palo Alto, Calif.

[89] See Daniel Verton, "The Threat From Within," Business2.0, April 1, 2000.

[90] United States of America v. Say Lye Ow, Plea Agreement, U.S. District Court, Northern District of California, San Jose Division, September 14, 2001.

[91] Kevin Poulsen, "Defendant: Microsoft source code sale was a setup," SecurityFocus, Nov. 11, 2004.

[92] These facts are based on transcripts of expert government witness testimony at the trial of U.S. v. Sullivan on April 19, 2001.

[93] USA v. Sullivan. 3:99CR122-v; Expert Opinion: Dr. John F. Repede, April 19, 2001.

[94] Ibid.

[95] Ibid.

[96] Some companies have reported that family members have surreptitiously submitted mom or dad's DNA (in the form of a hair, dead skin cell, toothbrush saliva etc..) to get to the bottom of family rumors of illness etc...

[97] Direct quote taken from recorded transcript of telephone conversation as outlined by Assistant U.S. Attorney Donald L. Hansen, Tampa Division, United States Attorney's Office for the Middle District of Florida, March 15, 2001.

[98] See www.sarbanes-oxley-101.com

[99] See Securities Industry Association,
http://www.sia.com/gramm_leach_bliley/

[100] See Robert H. Ledig, "Gramm-Leach-Bliley Act Financial Privacy Provisions: The Federal Government Imposes Broad Requirements to Address Consumer Privacy Concerns,"
http://www.ffhsj.com/bancmail/bmarts/ecdp_art.htm

INDEX

Printed in the United States
34566LVS00001B/1-66

9 781595 260307